The Naked Homeowner

Achieving Best Value in Buying or Selling Your Home

Peter Dolezal

Order this book online at www.trafford.com/07-0826
or email orders@trafford.com

Most Trafford titles are also available at major online book retailers.

Cover Design: Goodall Design, Victoria, BC.

Note for Librarians: A cataloguing record for this book is available from Library and Archives Canada at www.collectionscanada.ca/amicus/index-e.html

Printed in Victoria, BC, Canada.

ISBN: 978 1 4251-2521-9

www.trafford.com

North America & international
toll-free: 1 888 232 4444 (USA & Canada)
phone: 250 383 6864 • fax: 250 383 6804
email: info@trafford.com

The United Kingdom & Europe
phone: +44 (0)1865 722 113 • local rate: 0845 230 9601
facsimile: +44 (0)1865 722 868 • email: info.uk@trafford.com

10 9 8 7 6 5 4 3 2

CONTENTS

APPENDICES

INTRODUCTION

North Americans are among the most nomadic of people. With frequent changes of residence during his lifetime, the average person relocates about every five years.

Many of these moves involve the *sale* of one home and the *purchase* of another.

Typically, we start out by renting. As we progress through life economically, changing jobs and developing partnerships and families, we aspire to *own our home*, be it condo, townhouse, duplex, or single-family dwelling. Usually as family size and incomes increase we want, and need, larger homes. Then, when we become empty nesters, we often move into smaller, lower-maintenance homes, until age has us considering a final move to a senior's residence, with various levels of care.

This cycle often results in ten or more real estate transactions during our lifetime, each sale or purchase valued in the hundreds of thousands of dollars. Over the course of time, we may well have sold and bought homes with a cumulative value amounting to millions of dollars.

Our personal real estate holdings often account for the largest portion of our net worth. Of particular benefit to Canadian owners, are tax laws which permit any profits from selling a *primary* residence, to be fully exempt from taxes. This allows Canadians to take maximum advantage of increasing home values, to add dramatically to their net worth.

Increasing net worth is paramount for most of us, if we are to achieve financial independence, and maintain our lifestyle once we retire.

The effective management therefore, of the *process* of sale and purchase of the single largest asset most of us will ever own, should be a key priority of every homeowner. *IS IT ?*

In the 1990's, upon retirement from the corporate world, I was a founding partner of a very successful real estate company in Vancouver, BC, where I became personally involved in hundreds of, primarily residential, real estate transactions.

I found that many people with whom I dealt, were poorly prepared to manage effectively, the *sale and purchase process*, even in those cases where they had previously bought or sold a home.

I concluded that many of us expend much more effort in researching and purchasing an automobile or the latest media toy, than we do in handling our real estate transactions.

As a result, we often miss out on thousands of dollars of potential value.

....

In 2007 more than 500,000 residential sales are expected in Canada, most of them through the Multiple Listing Service (MLS). These sales will result in approximately one million individual home sales and purchases. Despite this huge annual volume of activity, there is a real dearth of information available on how to achieve best value in our residential real estate transactions.

This book aims to fill that void, and to provide an easy-to-read, step-by-step understanding of what we can, and should, be doing to maximize our financial benefit when buying or selling a home.

It is my hope that this information will encourage the reader to become much more effective and involved in his future sale or purchase transactions than he has been in the past. His enhanced knowledge and constructive participation should result in the achievement of better value and hence, greater net worth growth, over time.

An added benefit should be a significant reduction in the level of stress that is normally associated with any transaction valued in the hundreds of thousands of dollars.

....

Throughout the book I have consistently used the masculine, singular form to describe a Realtor, Buyer, Seller, Inspector, Lawyer or Notary. This is not due to any sexist bias, but rather is simply for the sake of convenience. I hope that the female half of the population will understand!

....

If you, the reader, follow through on the advice in this guide, you will have graduated from "Naked Homeowner," to an astute individual who can effectively manage the complex process of buying or selling his home, while at the same time achieving best value in each transaction.

Read on and....

HAVE FUN SELLING OR BUYING YOUR NEXT HOME!

PART I

LAYING THE GROUNDWORK:
PRELUDE TO BUYING OR SELLING

1. THE PRODUCT

2. THE MARKET ENVIRONMENT

THE PRODUCT

The residential real estate market can be characterized as vibrant and exciting, and at the same time, challenging and confusing. It serves up a virtual "banquet" of housing options, as varied and eclectic as the selection of products in your local supermarket.

Before delving into the processes and details of effective purchase or sale of our personal residence, let's first reflect on this huge array of options available to Buyers, and against which each Seller is competing.

What are some of the choices? Among the ***product mix*** available in the market, one can find:

- Mobile homes, on rented or owned pads
- Duplexes and other multiplexes, side-by-side or up-and-down
- Bare Land Strata homes, townhomes and duplexes
- Strata apartments, townhomes and duplexes
- Single-family dwellings, with or without rental suites
- Ranchers, split levels, and multi-storey homes
- Zero-lot-line properties
- Huge spectrum of lot sizes
- Acreage properties
- "Downtown" homes or "Suburbia"
- Farm properties
- Waterfront and view properties.

These are just the most typical examples.

As well as *product mix*, the real estate market also offers a broad range of ***pricing options***.

"Location, location, location!" How often have we heard that location is the primary driver of value?

Even within the same community, similar housing solutions can command huge differences in price. A modest house on a view or waterfront lot will attract a huge premium over a much better house in a more modest location.

Across Canada, we see average home prices for *comparable* housing products ranging from the low of $100,000 in many communities in the Maritimes, to $550,000 in Toronto and $650,000 in Vancouver.

....

How do these realities impact the Canadian Buyer or Seller?

1. The Buyer

Great news for the Buyer. His choice of quality, character, style and price of housing is limited only by his willingness to be mobile, to compromise on location both within his community and potentially across Canada. A Buyer needs to be aware of the value of the various trade-offs. For example:

a) A home's affordability is largely driven by lot size and location, both within a community, and between communities and provinces.

   Differences in construction cost between Sussex Corners, New Brunswick, and Toronto, for example, do exist. They are small however, in comparison to the land value on which the home is located. The difference in land values is not nearly as dramatic within a community itself, but even there, a *premium* location will attract a higher property value, and hence a higher home price.

b) A condominium will normally cost much less per square foot of accommodation than a single-family dwelling, due to a much more efficient use of land.

c) A townhome or duplex will usually cost more than a condominium apartment, due to the larger land footprint that it requires.

The Buyer with a limited budget can take comfort in the fact that these are options available to him when making a decision to buy a home, whether for the first time or as a replacement for a home he has sold.

The young graduate with no particular ties to any one area of Canada *can* decide to start his career in Winnipeg for example, and look forward to being able to afford a nice, single-family home within a year or two. His graduating friend, enamoured with Vancouver as his destination, will be lucky to afford, in the same time span, the purchase of a bachelor suite in a condominium complex.

The newly-retired couple with a home in Toronto or Vancouver is presented with a golden opportunity to enhance their retirement income. By selling in the higher-priced area, and buying in one of Canada's beautiful, less costly communities, they can improve their lifestyle, sometimes dramatically. Often this trade-off allows them to invest hundreds of thousands of dollars, due to the housing price difference.

Even within the same community, that same couple can bank a significant difference by moving to a smaller home, perhaps in a less expensive area.

REMEMBER..... Every Buyer of residential real estate has numerous choices and trade-offs to consider and from which to select, before launching a final search for his perfect housing solution.

The wise Buyer will take time to fully inform himself of the relative values of this smorgasbord of options available to him. In so doing, he can ensure that he achieves *best value for himself*, in return for his housing dollar.

2. The Seller

It is the astute Seller who keeps in mind the fact that the Buyers he is seeking to attract to his property, do have these numerous other choices.

A poorly presented, or overpriced, house will not sell easily. Because these choices exist for every Buyer, and they do exist in every community, the onus is on the Seller to choose a realistic value niche which is attractive to a significant number of potential Buyers.

Subsequent chapters deal at some length with the importance for Sellers, to properly prepare and present their home to the marketplace to *best advantage*, in order to cope effectively with the fierce competition for the Buyer dollar in the marketplace. Most importantly, they highlight the need for accurate pricing, and professional conduct of the complex process of selling a home.

REMEMBER..... It is not easy to fool the market on such a major expenditure. Buyers *will* compare and make trade-offs. It is the Seller who must ensure that *his* pricing, and marketing process, attracts Buyers.

....

Understanding the **product options,** and the trade-off opportunities within them, is important and useful to both Buyer and Seller. Equally important, is understanding the **market environment**, within which we hope to buy or sell a home.

The next section will assist in achieving that understanding.

MARKET ENVIRONMENT

Whether planning to buy or sell a home, you will find it very useful to first understand the residential real estate market environment in which you hope to be successful.

Although you are likely to retain a real estate professional to help you succeed, you must *yourself* be reasonably tuned in to the market if you are to manage effectively, the entire process, including that of choosing your Realtor.

BUYER'S MARKET? SELLER'S MARKET? BALANCED MARKET?

One hears these terms often, but what do they mean? How do we determine which we are experiencing? How must we modify our strategy to participate in the market which exists at the time?

1. BUYER'S MARKET

In a Buyer's Market the Buyer is king.
We will typically see the following:

- the number of listings is increasing and is significantly higher than a year earlier;
- the number of home sales is declining relative to previous periods;
- the average selling period is lengthening, and probably exceeds 120 days;
- the average and, more importantly, the median, selling price of homes is falling.

The Buyer should be able to achieve excellent value, since there will be much more product from which to choose. Sellers will be more anxious, and hence more flexible, on price and other contract terms. The Seller will face stiff competition from other Sellers, as well as a shortage of potential Buyers.

In the face of this reality, the Seller's choice of Realtor becomes most critical. The marketing program for his home must be effective. Most important, the pricing must be spot-on at worst, or even slightly below market, if he is to achieve a successful and timely sale.

In a prolonged Buyer's Market, the number of active Realtors in the area will decline, as economic realities force the marginally successful ones to seek other, more secure sources of income.

2. SELLER'S MARKET

In a Seller's Market, the exact reverse of the above conditions will exist.

If his home is well-priced, the Seller will be in the driver's seat. Buyers may have to move fast on their first choice to avoid being scooped by others. They may even have to participate in multiple offers on the same property. And generally, it is the Buyer who will have to show the greater flexibility in the contract he seeks to finalize on his target home.

A Seller's Market will often be characterized by:

- the average listing selling within 45 to 60 days;
- a significant, upward movement in prices;
- a declining number of listings;
- selling prices at close to listing prices;
- increasing incidence of multiple offers;
- an increase in the number of Realtors.

3. BALANCED MARKET

In a Balanced Market, the bargaining power of both Buyer and Seller is roughly equal.

Characteristics of a **Balanced Market** will include:

- a healthy number of listings on the market;
- a steady and fairly consistent turnover of listings;
- an average listing period before sale, of 60 to 120 days;
- relatively stable median and average selling prices.

....

In reality however, the Market will rarely sit precisely at one of these three states.

It will shift on a continuum trending toward a seller's market, a buyer's market, or balance. Roughly where it rests at any point in time along this scale, is vital information. Every Buyer or Seller should have at least an approximate appreciation of this, before venturing into the market place.

4. DETERMINING THE STATE OF THE MARKET

How do we acquire this information? Most of us are not professionals in the real estate business.

The task may at first glance seem daunting and time consuming. It is, in fact, very easily obtained, and in very little time.

There are approximately 100 Real Estate Boards in Canada. For virtually every area of the country, you will find a Multiple Listing Service (MLS) website.

Many communities also produce a weekly or bi-weekly publication which lists all advertised properties in the area. Each month in that same publication, you will likely find a summary by the President of the local Real Estate Board, of the state of the market in the most recent month, with a comparison to the previous month and year. It will usually indicate total listings, number of sales, average and median prices and, in the larger centres, a sales price and volume breakdown by area.

Additionally, your local newspaper will often summarize such data monthly and provide interpretation, which helps to categorize the *general market condition in your area.*

If you watch for, and study, these hard statistical indicators for a month or two before entering the market, you will be reasonably tuned in to the type of market which exists. This information will help you to intelligently assess and discuss specific marketing strategies with your spouse, or ultimately with a potential or selected Realtor.

While an understanding of the condition of the market is key, it is by no means the only information you need before jumping into the sale or purchase process.

What else do we need? Again, the list may be daunting, but broken down into simple elements, the answers can be found in relatively short order. In fact, it can all be done simultaneously with the state-of-the-market assessment described above.

Chapters One and Eleven address in some detail, these additional issues for respectively, the Seller and the Buyer.

PART II

THE SELLING PROCESS

CHAPTER ONE

ISSUES FOR THE SELLER

- Is the Seller pressed to sell or can he take his time?
- What are the facts on any remaining mortgage on his home?
- Objectively, what is the current condition of his house?
- What is the realistic cost of selling, relocating, and establishing in a new home?

Until a potential Seller understands, and can answer, these questions, he really should not begin the sale process. Even if his house sells, he may receive a shock when the actual *net* proceeds are tallied, and he receives far less than he may have imagined.

Unless one is involved in a job relocation or other forced event, going through this process will allow the homeowner to objectively *determine whether selling his home is really the right decision at a particular time.*

A potential Seller must be certain of that answer *before* he starts interviewing and selecting Realtors!

Let's address these issues one at a time.

1. THE NEED TO SELL

- ***If the Seller must sell***, and relatively quickly due to a job change, economic circumstances, family break-up, or other imperatives, he will have no choice but to move forward with the process fairly quickly. He should nevertheless, determine the answers to each of the aforementioned questions before proceeding, in order to do so intelligently, and without false expectations.

- The Seller who is ***not pressed to sell***, but instead, is planning to upgrade, upsize, downsize or simply change location, and to whom it matters little whether he does so in the next three months or a year, is in a much better position to achieve optimum value from his property. Furthermore, he can be far more relaxed about the process, and relatively philosophical, should the answers to these questions suggest that selling may be premature.

Ideally, one always wants to be in the second category, but sometimes realities dictate otherwise. We must be prepared to cope, and to achieve best possible value in either circumstance.

2. MORTGAGE STATUS

If the Seller is to effectively calculate the financial result of selling, and determine how much he can afford to spend on a new home, he *must* have a clear picture of his present mortgage status, namely:

- What is the remaining principal balance?
- Is the mortgage portable, and without penalty, to a new home?
- Based on the Seller's family income, debts and net worth, by how much incrementally, will the Lender allow the Seller to increase his mortgage on a replacement home?
- What is the present interest rate on any incremental mortgage amount, and by how much would that increase the Seller's existing monthly payments?

The answers to these questions are easily obtainable at a brief meeting with your Mortgage Lender. Typical information you will have to provide is your household's assets, total income, debts, and monthly payments. With that in hand, the Lender can give you a very precise approximation of your status and eligibility for additional mortgage funds. Often the Lender will offer you this information in the form of a ***pre-approval***, the terms of which will protect you from any interest rate increases, usually for a period of 60 to 120 days.

Carefully examine the information the Lender gives you. Make sure, if you have the option, that it really *does* make sense to proceed with listing your home. Clearly, if the amount of mortgage for which you qualify does not allow you to purchase the calibre of home that you wish to own, then perhaps you should put your plans on the back burner until you pay down other debts, your family income increases, or both.

See "More on Mortgages" in Part IV.

3. CURRENT HOME CONDITION

Walk around the interior and exterior of your home, pencil and paper in hand, pretending you are a potential Buyer. Note each and every physical defect that might deter you from buying this home. Write down everything. It does not mean you are going to fix every item before listing, but it provides a starting point for making decisions on what you really should repair or clean up before proceeding further.

Your review should include:

- Roof and eaves condition;
- Exterior and interior paint condition;
- Failed window seals;
- Signs of insects and other pests;
- Working condition of furnace, hot water tank, plumbing, and appliances;
- State of your landscaping, driveway and walkways.

If, for instance, the roof is on its last legs, you are not likely to spend $15,000 to replace it before listing, nor would I suggest you do. But, in noting its condition, it will be a reminder that your potential listing price will have to be attractive enough to a Buyer to allow him to budget a substantial sum for a new roof, within a few years of buying your home.

On the other hand, if your review highlights that by spending $1500 to replace a broken seal on a high-profile window, buy some paint and take a week to touch up or repaint parts of the house, and hire a professional exterminator to get rid of carpenter ant activity, you certainly should do so. Even should you end up *not* listing your home, these are necessary maintenance items which should be done to maintain the value of your investment.

4. COST OF SELLING

Many people listing their home for sale fail to estimate accurately, ***the real cost of selling***. They start the process with rose-coloured glasses, often greatly overestimating the final *net* proceeds of an eventual sale.

Let's examine the real, likely costs, using for our example, $400,000 as an estimated selling price:

a) Preparation Costs

Let's assume that **$1500** is our estimated cost for readying our home for sale.

b) Commission Costs

This figure will vary slightly from area to area, and is in fact, negotiable with the Realtor you eventually select.

An "exclusive" listing usually results in a slightly lower commission because the Realtor hopes to not have to share it with another Realtor. However, because it *is* exclusive, your home will *not* be included on the Multiple Listing Service (MLS) and will as a result, receive more limited exposure.

The greatest majority of homes for sale in Canada today are listed on the MLS, as is the case in our example.

MLS listing commission *benchmarks* will vary somewhat across Canada. In the Vancouver area for example, the benchmark is 7% on the first $100,000 of sale value and 2.5% on the balance. In Victoria this changes to 6% on the first $100,000 of value and 3% on the balance. In Toronto it's a flat 5% of selling price. In Montreal it is 6%.

We'll assume a Victoria location; hence we apply the "6 and 3%" commission guideline. In our $400,000 sale price example therefore, the commission would be **$15,000** ($6,000 + $9,000), plus GST of **$900,** for a total of **$15,900.**

c) Legal Costs

Again, these will vary somewhat, depending on which Notary or Lawyer you choose, and on the complexity of your transaction. It's a safe approximation to use **$1000** as a typical legal cost.

d) Closing Adjustments

There may be utility and miscellaneous other cost adjustments, that the Lawyer or Notary will calculate in detail, after a sale occurs. The main item to consider in our estimate of costs is a potential **property tax** obligation.

Most property taxes are due on July 1. Any adjustment owed by, or due to, a Seller is calculated on a calendar-year basis. If you complete a sale *before* paying your property taxes on July 1, you will owe the Buyer the pro-rated portion of your taxes, equal to the proportion of time you lived in your home during the calendar year before the actual sale completed.

On the other hand, if the sale closing date falls *after* July 1, the Buyer will owe you that portion of the taxes which you had prepaid for the period of his occupancy after July 1.

Rather than get caught up in difficult calculations, especially not knowing when your house will actually sell (you have not, as yet, even firmly decided to list), I suggest you use one half of your property tax bill to cover an estimate of all unexpected costs. Let's assume your annual taxes on this $400,000 home are $3000. You would then use **$1500** in your estimate. You won't be out by much once the dust settles.

e) Moving Costs

You will have a pretty good feel for whether you plan to have your friends or family help you move, or if you plan to use a moving company. Renting a truck and buying your friends dinner may limit your cost to a few hundred dollars.

On the other hand, a moving company could cost you in the thousands of dollars. You can call up any reputable moving company and request an estimate for a truck and four men for a move within town. For a typical household, this cost will probably be in the $1500 to $2000 range, assuming you do your own packing.

It's a little more complex if you are relocating to another region of the province or country because such moves are generally priced on a weight (per 1000 lbs.) and distance basis. The moving company may suggest a visit to your home to give you an accurate estimate, after listing all your possessions.

For purposes of our example, let's assume you are moving within town, that you will rent a truck, and have friends help. This should limit your cost to no more than **$500.**

....

These five cost estimates will clearly have a major impact on your *net* proceeds from a sale. In summary they are:

• **Preparation**	**$ 1,500**
• **Commission**	**$ 15,900**
• **Legal**	**$ 1,000**
• **Adjustments**	**$ 1,500**
• **Moving**	**$ 500**
Total Estimated Costs of Selling and Moving:	**$ 20,400**

REMEMBER..... The above estimate reflects only the selling and moving costs. It does not include the additional costs associated with purchasing a replacement home, if that is your plan.

Purchase costs will be dealt with in a later Chapter.

CHAPTER TWO

ESTIMATING VALUES & THE DECISION TO SELL

In Chapter One we illustrated how a potential Seller can arrive at a realistic cost estimate for selling his home and moving. We used a $400,000 selling price as the starting point of our calculations.

But how does our potential Seller arrive at an approximation of his home's sale value? He must be reasonably accurate, in order to calculate an estimate of the **net proceeds** of a sale. It is from this calculation that he will determine if selling at this time is a prudent course of action.

For preliminary decision purposes this is not only fairly easy, but also fun!

1. STEPS TO REACHING AN ESTIMATE

a) Look up your local Multiple Listing Service website. All listed MLS properties in your target market can be found at "mls.ca".

b) Read your local real estate publication.

c) Examine the listing price of homes that are of similar size and general characteristics as yours, such as age, location, and views.

d) Take note of how long it appears to take for listings to sell.

e) Track down the selling price of every home that has sold in your neighbourhood in the recent past. Some provinces such as British Columbia make this information readily available through their *Assessment Authority* website. If all else fails, call the Realtor who had listed the particular home. He will be happy to tell you its selling price.

f) Take every opportunity to visit open houses in your area to obtain a feel for your area's values. The added benefit of this is that you will meet some of the Realtors who work in your area. This will give you a sense of their personality, marketing program and sales technique – useful if you eventually make the decision to list. *More on this in a subsequent Chapter.*

g) Look at your *Property Tax Assessment*, which is meant to be a very rough approximation of market value.

h) Consider commissioning, at your expense, an independent appraisal by a professional Appraiser. The $300 or so that it costs may well be worth it in order to establish a realistic benchmark price for your calculations.

If the above process does not give you a result with which you are comfortable, feel free to call one or two successful Realtors in your area. Ask them for an evaluation. They will be happy to do this for you as long as you return the courtesy and give them consideration, if and when, you later decide to list. Remember that any evaluation you receive from a Realtor or Appraiser will have a *shelf life* of perhaps three months.

2. CALCULATION OF APPROXIMATE NET PROCEEDS OF A SALE

Assume for our example, that having gone through this process, we have determined that $400,000 is a reasonable estimate of our selling price.

We can now use this figure as the starting point for our calculations which will lead us to an approximation of our Seller's **net** proceeds from a $400,000 sale. The results will help us determine whether it makes sense to list at this time.

Estimated Selling Price :		$ 400,000
Subtract previously estimated Selling Costs:		
• Home preparation costs	$ 1,500	
• Commission costs	$ 15,900	
• Legal costs	$ 1,000	
• Miscellaneous closing costs	$ 1,500	
• Moving costs	$ 500	
		$ 20,400

Net Estimated Proceeds of Sale **$ 379,600**

3. MORTGAGE ELIGIBILITY

The expected *net proceeds of a sale* is key information the Seller needs.

Equally vital however, to determining whether this would allow him to buy the next home of his dreams, is to factor in the amount of mortgage for which he would qualify.

Hopefully you, the prospective Seller, will previously have learned from your Mortgage Lender:

- The outstanding balance of your existing mortgage;
- Whether it is portable to a new home without penalty;
- How much mortgage incrementally, the Lender would allow you to borrow for a new home, and at what rate;
- The total amount of your new *blended* monthly payment on the maximum borrowing.

Let's assume that this earlier investigation of the mortgage resulted in the following information:

- The outstanding mortgage principal on your existing home is $202,000; it is portable without penalty to a new home;
- Based on your household income and total debt obligations, you qualify for an incremental mortgage of $153,000;
- Should you end up using this full extra amount, your present payments would increase by about $975 per month.

4. DRAWING CONCLUSIONS

a) Your present equity in your home is approximately $198,000 ($400,000, minus the $202,000 mortgage principal remaining).

b) Your Lender would likely allow you to buy a replacement home for as much as $532,600 (your $379,600 net selling price, plus the $153,000 incremental loan).

CAUTION! YOU WILL INCUR *ADDITIONAL BUYING COSTS* ON YOUR NEXT HOME.

As a result, this $532,600 maximum purchase price eligibility will have to be reduced by about $8,000 due to the costs you will incur when *buying* your new home. *(See subsequent section on "Buying Costs")*

c) Your adjusted maximum purchase price would become approximately $525,000 ($532,600 minus $8,000).

d) Because you are not as yet, even at the listing stage, be ultra-conservative. Reduce this estimate by another $25,000, to allow for market slippage on the sale of your home.

This means that you can be reasonably safe in planning to invest up to $500,000 to purchase a replacement home, *if* your present home sells successfully, for a worst-case price, of only $375,000.

5. THE DECISION: TO SELL? OR NOT SELL?

The last important questions which you, the prospective Seller, must now ask yourself, are:

a) Based on your general knowledge of what $500,000 can buy in the current market, can you expect to meet your size, location and other objectives in the purchase of a replacement home?

b) Do you feel comfortable with the prospect of adding up to $975 to your present, regular monthly expenditures?

If you feel totally confident, and can answer in the affirmative to both of these questions, you are ready to list your house!

....

YOU'VE DONE YOUR HOMEWORK TO ENSURE THAT LISTING, AT THIS TIME, IS INDEED A SOUND DECISION.

CHAPTER THREE

LET'S LIST!

Now that we are certain that listing our home for sale is a good decision, it's time to answer a few quick, remaining questions:

- Timing of listing?
- Private sale? Or Realtor listing?
- How to find a superior Realtor?

1. TIMING

Job relocation, or other pressures to list immediately, may give you little choice but to proceed right away. However, if you *do* have a choice on timing, consider this.

Generally, November and December see the lowest inventory of listings. This time of year therefore, may produce surprising levels of Buyer interest. There are always Buyers looking, and with limited product choice available to them, you may be surprised at the number of showings you attract, especially if you are well-located.

On the other hand, in many parts of Canada at that time of year, your home will not present well if buried in snow!

Spring *may* be a better time to list. There will be some pent-up demand from those who were too preoccupied to shop for homes at year-end. Now that days are getting longer, dressing up the exterior of your home for an early spring display can be fun, and your home should show well. You *will* face heavier competition however, because springtime is usually when inventories of listed homes will rise sharply.

Also keep in mind that families often want to sell, buy, and settle into a new home before school re-opens in September.

These are points to consider *if* you have the option to pick and choose when you list.

Otherwise, go for it! List, and do the very best job you can, in managing the process, whatever the time of year.

2. PRIVATE SALE? OR RETAIN A REALTOR?

Almost everyone will ask, "Why give a Realtor $15,000 or more of my home price? Why shouldn't I try to sell the house myself, and save this large expense?"

The short answer *generally*, is,

DON'T TRY TO SELL BY YOURSELF!

While there are exceptions to every rule, this one included, attempting the sale process by yourself is a gamble in which the odds are stacked against you.

WHY?

Would you try to defend yourself in a court of law? Would you try to be your own doctor? Obviously not! Real estate is also a profession, in which the training and experience of a ***good*** Realtor should translate into ***better results*** for the Seller.

A Realtor will spend a great deal of time and money in marketing your home. If not, you have chosen the wrong Realtor – *but we'll come to that later!*

Selling your home *successfully* will require much hard work and careful implementation of a *comprehensive marketing plan*, including:

- Exposing your home to a broad audience which can directly influence success. A professional Realtor can put your home on the **Multiple Listing Service**. You can not. This ensures that every Realtor in your market area has knowledge of, and exposure to, your home. Because other Realtors would receive about one half of the total commission, they will have significant incentive to bring your home to the attention of their potential Buyers.

- Preparation of photographs, brochures, exact floor plans, and advertising, may well run into several thousand dollars over the course of your listing. Are you willing to arrange this, expending the necessary funds, and do you have the time and expertise to do so to your home's best advantage?
- Are you prepared to personally promote and hold open houses, *and* not react inappropriately to various comments your home may receive?
- Upon receiving an offer, are you prepared and able to properly negotiate, document and execute the necessary documents in a manner that protects you legally, while still achieving best value for you, the Seller?

The odds are that a potential Buyer will have retained an experienced Realtor to represent his interests. A good Realtor, working on *your* behalf, should be able to level the playing field, and minimize the risk of the Buyer gaining the upper hand.

If you choose the right Realtor, his experience and training should translate into a well-documented and legally-enforceable sale, as well as better value for you, the Seller, than is likely if you try to sell by yourself.

Accurate pricing is always key to a successful and relatively quick sale. With only limited knowledge of the market place, how will you be sure that you have not priced yourself out of the market, *or* priced too low, leaving money on the table?

It is important to realize that generally, a Buyer who likes a home which is "For Sale by Owner" will expect a deal! He knows you are avoiding paying a commission, and he will expect to grab as much of that saving as he can, thereby eroding your potential gain.

Except in a very hot Seller's Market, the reduced exposure typically experienced in a *"By Owner"* sales effort will greatly reduce your chance of selling. At the very least, it will add significantly to the time required to find a Buyer.

Some of you may agree in principle, but still want to find a compromise approach that can save you money. In most areas of the country, options exist which will provide *some* framework for you to list and sell your own home, for costs ranging from a few hundred, to several thousand dollars.

Additionally, in some areas of Canada, organizations exist such as "One Percent Realty". Listing with them will get your home on the MLS system and you *can* save significantly on your commission cost. **Remember however, that in these cases, the *one percent* applies only to the listing agent's commission**. Other Realtors will know that you may choose to decline paying them the traditional selling commission, and will therefore be less likely to show your home. Clearly this reduces your home's exposure to showings. In a very strong Seller's Market your risk is less, but regardless of the market, you have to decide if the trade-off you are making is worth it.

While caution is in order when using any discount sales vehicle, this approach is certainly better than flying totally on your own. Do however, remember the axiom....

"You generally get what you pay for!"

....

At this point, some of you may be thinking that this author is obviously an avid lobbyist for Realtors! Not true. Not for all Realtors. But for the truly good Realtors, I am a strong advocate, because they should be able to deliver far more added value for the Seller, than the cost incurred in retaining them.

Let me conclude my comments on this point with an observation from my own experience.

As previously mentioned, I was a successful Realtor with my own company in Vancouver, BC. I personally sold as many as 60 homes in a year. This placed me consistently in the top one or two percent of some 9500 Lower Mainland, BC, Realtors, in both performance and earnings.

Yet, despite this extensive experience and a proven track record, when it was recently our turn to sell and buy another home, we did not hesitate. We located the best possible Realtor in our area and retained him. We not only partnered with him successfully, but also had no regrets whatsoever, about his earning the full, standard commission.

That's the best evidence I can offer, about how strongly I feel that, generally, one should not try to act as his own Realtor!

3. THE REALTOR SELECTION PROCESS

In 2006, approximately 88,000 Realtors across Canada sold some 340,000 MLS listed homes. That on average, is only about four MLS homes per Realtor!

This means that the *average Realtor* would have been lucky to gross $40,000 for his entire year's work. Hardly a fortune! Especially since such earnings are *before* the many costs he must incur as a Realtor.

Despite this statistic, from my experience in the market, it is about 25% of Realtors who account for some 80% of the sales, and hence earn 80% of the commissions! It is from this elite group of Realtors, which exists in every area of Canada, that the prudent Seller (or Buyer) will want to *shop* for his ideal choice to represent his interests.

Selecting the right Realtor is crucial to your success, not only in selling, but also in maximizing your selling price.

Why would you settle for anything less than the best? You need not!

REMEMBER.... It costs no more to hire an exceptional Realtor than a mediocre one!

So How Do We Choose the Best Possible Realtor? We:

- Do our research – who are the achievers?
- Screen the candidates.
- Invite evaluation and marketing proposals.
- Select the best choice.

a) Your Research

Become familiar with those Realtors who consistently list and sell in *your* general area. What is the point of selecting someone who works primarily in the city core, if you live in the suburbs, or vice versa?

You want a Realtor who knows, and can sell your neighbourhood, as well as your home within it.

- **Area Listings**
  Go on line. Pick up your area publication which lists homes for sale. Become familiar with listings in your general area. Note those Realtors who advertise regularly and well. Keep an eye on their turnover of listings. If their listings are selling reasonably quickly, they are obviously doing something correctly.

  Keep in mind that "high-end" listings will often take much longer to sell, due to the very limited number of Buyers in this market segment.

  On the other hand, you may spot a Realtor who has "stale" listings, with prices being reduced a number of times. This *may* be a Realtor who attracts listings by quoting Sellers an irresistibly high price. Or it may be that the Seller insisted on an unrealistically high listing price. In either case, that Realtor allowed the situation to arise.

- **Open Houses**
  Go to every open house you can, in your general area. Not only will you enhance your feel for prices, and for homes against which yours will be competing, but just as important, you will meet the Realtors whom you may be thinking of inviting to make a proposal for listing your own home.

  Engage the Realtor in a discussion about the home you are visiting. Form an opinion on how professional and knowledgeable he is, about both the home and the area. You will also be able to sense how his style and personality may fit your expectations. Examine the brochure that he hands out. Does it contain a professional floor plan, attractive photos, and key information on the house?

....

Some Realtors may tell you that open houses are a waste of time, and that they do not work.

From my personal experience, of hundreds of successful sales of listed homes, I can confirm that ***open houses, properly promoted and conducted, do work****. I kept track over the years and found that approximately 24% of my listings sold as a direct result of open houses.*

It *is* true that some Realtors do not find open houses to be very successful. I believe that this is more a reflection on their technique, than on the basic value of holding an open house.

Unless I were selling a *very high-value* home, generally over $1 million, I would think very hard before selecting a Realtor who tried to convince me that open houses are not a key component of an effective marketing program. They almost always are!

b) Screening The Candidate Realtors

Let's assume that you have identified two or three Realtors who fit the above general criteria. Invite each, individually, to visit your home when both you and your spouse will be available. Tell them that you would appreciate an evaluation, as well as a comprehensive listing proposal. Spread the visits out over a two or three day period so that you can spend an hour or two with each potential Realtor.

After each Realtor's visit, compare notes with your partner on your general impressions:

- Did the Realtor *listen* to your needs and concerns?
- Did he answer your questions clearly and well?
- Did he take the time to *really* examine your home?
- Did you both "click" with his personality and style?

All of these are important considerations for you to take into account once you receive the Realtor's evaluation and marketing proposal.

A worksheet in Appendix 1 may help with your evaluation, ranking, and selection process. Customize it to fully reflect what you believe to be important.

Most Realtors will wish to take a few days to do their own research, and to document a proposal for you. They will ask when they may return to present it to you. This is normal and desirable. You don't want a snap opinion, or a verbal proposal. You are looking for a professional, written presentation, that you can take the time to digest, and to compare to the other proposals you expect to receive

c) The Realtor's Proposal

The ideal proposal should address at least the following:

- Proposed listing and selling price range;
- Detailed logic for the recommended listing price;
- The proposed commission structure, and its competitiveness;
- Information about the general market, and the competition specific to your area;
- Information on the Realtor's company, and his personal success history in selling homes;
- Scope and timing of a promotional brochure on your home;
- Details on the proposed marketing program, which should include:
    - Frequency, type and location of advertising;
    - Frequency of open houses;
    - Open house plan for Realtors;
    - Website: quality, content, and promotion value.

When meeting with the Realtor, be sure to test *his* listing price recommendations against the estimate at which *you* had earlier arrived, based on your preliminary research.

REMEMBER..... Beware the Realtor whose proposed price is clearly above any reasonable estimate of market value!

That Realtor may be trying to entice you to list at an attractive price, knowing full well that he will, some time after listing, have to urge you to make substantial reductions.

You want and need a professional Realtor who can clearly prove his recommendations, and who recommends a listing value that usually ends up within a few percent of the actual selling price.

Be alert also, to those Realtors who urge you to list on the *low* side of the market. While this may achieve a quick sale, with little expenditure of time or money by the Realtor, it is not necessarily *in your best interest.*

If you *do* need a quick sale for personal reasons, you might agree to list on the low end of the market range, but do so only after the Realtor commits to a major, supporting marketing program which will boost your chances of not only a quick sale, but also one that is very close to your listing price.

The better option may be the Realtor who provides a potential listing *range* with a lower and an upper figure, with good supporting information. He would then invite you to choose a listing price within that range, after informing you of the ramifications of your various choices.

That min/max range might be a maximum spread of 5%. Should you choose to try the upper limit, you may wish to agree at the time of listing, that should this higher-end price not attract significant traffic of potential Buyers within the first four or five weeks, you will support the downward adjustment of the listing price at that time.

If the prospective Realtor falls short of your expectations on his marketing program, challenge him on it; see if he will change the proposal, or if he can convince you that he is correct.

REMEMBER... ***You* are hiring this individual and entrusting him with the sale of what is likely your most valuable asset. You have a right to be thoroughly convinced that his proposal has the greatest possible chance of delivering best value for you.**

Keep in mind that anyone with a rudimentary knowledge of computers can crank out a 30-page, nicely-bound package, and do so in an hour! I'd rather see a brief, but thorough, well-thought-out, and clearly presented proposal which addresses each of my expectations as a Seller.

Do not be mesmerized by the slickness of the Realtor's presentation package. Scrutinize the detailed content, not the glossiness!

d) Making Your Selection

Hopefully, you will have gone through the above process with a minimum of two, or possibly three, Realtors. You will have received, and reviewed with each, their presentation, and will have promised to get back to them in a few days' time.

Take the time to sit down for a quiet hour or two with your partner, and together review each proposal. Compare the strengths and weaknesses of each. Again, don't let yourself be drawn automatically to the Realtor offering the highest listing price. Review his, and the other proponents' market information to see if that price really is supportable.

If you have pre-selected your candidates well, there should not be a huge discrepancy in the recommended listing prices. They are, after all, using the same data to justify their recommendations!

Often, you will find that your decision is driven by factors other than the suggested listing price. The quality of the marketing program, the work ethic, and the competence of the Realtor, are probably more important than hitting the ideal listing price spot-on!

One extremely important consideration is the degree to which your prospective Realtor embraces and uses new technology to its full potential. A Realtor without for instance, a high-quality website, is working at a huge disadvantage to those who maintain a sophisticated and successful one. A Seller needs to satisfy himself that his listing will have the full benefit of this proven marketing tool.

Try to achieve a clear consensus with your partner on which Realtor is best for you. Who has given you the greatest confidence that he can achieve your selling objectives?

If you can not seem to agree, or if you both are uncomfortable with all of the proposals, perhaps you need to start over, and invite proposals from other candidates. Take heart, this rarely is necessary.

Once you have together made a clear decision, again invite the successful Realtor to your home to discuss and finalize a **Listing Agreement**.

Remember also, to call the unsuccessful Realtors, to thank them for their efforts, and advise them of your decision. They now know your home, and may well bring a Buyer to view it, even if you have listed with someone else. You certainly would want them to do so!

CHAPTER FOUR

THE LISTING AGREEMENT

The Realtor you have chosen will now return with a formal Listing Agreement for you to sign. This is the first of a number of *legal documents* to which you will be exposed in the sale process. It is important that you understand its contents, and not sign blindly.

The Listing Agreement is a legal contract between the home Seller and the Realtor. In addition to the routine identification of owners, address and legal site description, it will contain the following items:

- Listing Price
- Listing Duration
- Commission Structure
- Chattels and Fixtures
- Signatures & Property Condition Disclosure

Let's review each of these:

1. LISTING PRICE

This will be the dollar amount that you and the Realtor have agreed is the value at which he will be promoting your home for sale.

2. LISTING DURATION

The Realtor will prefer the longest possible period for the listing, because it binds the owner to him for the entire duration. It also increases the probability that the home will sell during that lengthy time frame.

From a homeowner's perspective, you want to give the Realtor a reasonable listing period, long enough for him to sell your home, if he is as effective as he led you to believe when he made his initial proposal to secure your listing. On the other hand, should he not prove effective after a reasonable time frame, you want to be free to change Realtors.

Most Real Estate Boards will require that the listing period be a minimum of 60 days. It is reasonable to agree to a Realtor's request for a listing period of 90 to 120 days in the case of an *average-priced* home. For *high-end* homes which need exposure to a wider, perhaps even global market, a 180-day listing period would be reasonable.

Obviously, during this three-to-four month period you, the Seller, will have had a great deal of first-hand experience with your Realtor.

If, at the end of the listing period, your home has not sold, you will be able to make a reasoned judgement whether it is due to the Realtor's shortcomings, the state of the market, your price level, or a combination of these factors.

If you are satisfied that the reason is not the Realtor himself, and that he has worked hard and well on your behalf, you may well decide to extend the listing. Any such extension would normally be for a shorter period, often 30 to 60 days.

3. COMMISSION STRUCTURE

The Realtor will propose a commission structure, usually that which prevails in that market place. It will often be 6 to 7% on the first $100,000 of sale value, and 2½ to 3% on the balance. If we continue to use a $400,000 sale price as our example, in a "6 and 3%" market area, then the commission payable by you on the sale would be:

6% of $100,000	– $ 6,000
3% of $300,000	– $ 9,000
	$15,000
GST (6%)	$ 900
TOTAL	$ 15,900

The Listing Agreement should also set out the amount of commission payable to the *selling* Realtor, should he be *other* than your own Realtor. This figure will vary from just slightly less than 50% of the commission, to a full 50%. The closer this number is to 50%, the better for you. As a Seller, you want to be sure that a reasonable percentage is offered to other Realtors, to ensure they have sufficient incentive to bring their clients to view your home.

REMEMBER.......Commissions *are* negotiable!

However, any agreement you make with *your Realtor* on varying *his* commission, should be done by means of a ***side agreement*** between you and your Realtor. You must *not* change the terms in the Listing Agreement, to avoid affecting other Realtors negatively. Realtors will lose interest in your listing if they see that their commission on *your* house would be lower than that on others.

Again, keep in mind that you do get what you pay for!

A wise homeowner must be careful to not squeeze his listing Realtor's commission unreasonably, while still expecting all of the costly services that the Realtor laid out in his original proposal, and which drew you to him in the first place.

Really good Realtors will not be interested in accepting drastic commission cuts because they know that full implementation of their marketing plan will be expensive.

Despite these cautions, *side agreements* which should result in a winning formula for both parties, can be made on the listing Realtor's commission rates.

For example, I routinely offered Sellers who listed with me, a **side letter** which included the following undertakings:

a) Should the home sell without the assistance of another Realtor (a transaction known as a "Double Ender"), the commission structure set out in the Listing Agreement, would be reduced by $2,000 or $3,000, depending on the value of the home.

b) Should the Seller purchase a replacement home, utilizing my services to do so, *prior to completion* of the sale of his home, the listing commission would be reduced by $1,000.

AND

c) Should both of these events occur, the Seller would benefit from *both* reductions.

I found that homeowners almost always considered this to be a fair sharing of the benefits. And from my perspective as a Realtor, it was a useful way to ensure that I retained my client's interest in my services when he went looking for a replacement home, often on his own at open houses. A true win-win situation!

Appendix 2 is a draft letter setting out the framework for such a side agreement.

> **REMEMBER..... While both parties potentially benefit, a side agreement should *not* change the commission entitlement of other Realtors, thereby maintaining their full incentive for selling your home.**

If, before you sign the Listing Agreement, your Realtor does not offer you an arrangement along these lines, make the suggestion yourself. You will find most Realtors to be receptive.

4. CHATTELS AND FIXTURES

It is important that you make clear in your Listing Agreement which ***chattels***, if any, you wish to include in your sale, as well as which ***fixtures*** you wish to take with you, hence excluding them from the sale.

*The general definition of a **chattel** includes those items which are portable contents and not attached to the home structure.*

This would include, for instance, furniture, stand-alone appliances, paintings, draperies, and area rugs. It is strictly within *your* discretion, to include any chattel in the sale. The chattels which Sellers will most frequently decide to include in the sale, are appliances and window coverings.

Fixtures, with a few exceptions, normally remain with the home. As the name implies, *a **fixture** is an item which is an integral part of the home*, such as a hot tub, furnace, hot water tank, cabinets and wall-mounted mirrors.

To some homeowners' surprise, drapery rods, towel racks, and light bulbs are also considered fixtures.

The fixture that homeowners most frequently wish to exclude from the sale is a chandelier.

A Realtor can provide guidance on what is normally considered an included fixture. Not all items however, can be clearly categorized. What about the 6' x 4' mirror that is mounted in your foyer, or the large bird bath and the huge concrete flower pots in your garden? If you are really attached to any of these items, identify and specify *each, in writing,* as being excluded.

REMEMBER..... If you go overboard in excluding too many items, you may be diminishing the sale-ability of your home.

If the $1200 mirror in your foyer is the focal point of that area, and if the lawn ornaments really complement your garden, it may be to your advantage to leave them as inclusions, then buy replacement ones when you move.

The important point to keep in mind is that from the outset, ambiguity must be eliminated, to avoid the risk of disputes after a sale, or even the loss of a potential sale during negotiations.

The mere documentation of a key inclusion or exclusion in the Listing Agreement does not bind you irrevocably when you receive an offer. For example, a particular Buyer may find it more beneficial to negotiate a slightly lower price on your home, than to have your expensive mirror or collection of garden pots. These facts may well be considered by both parties during the negotiations.

All you have really done in the Listing Agreement, is to equip your Realtor with the specifics of what you *prefer* to include or exclude. He will convey that information, in documentation to his Real Estate Board, so that in turn, it is made available to potential Buyers through their own Realtors.

It is the wise Seller, and his Realtor, who pay very careful attention to being crystal clear, BUT also reasonable, on this very important issue.

It is worth noting that some Sellers may be willing to part with some of their major **chattels,** perhaps because they are downsizing.

If you are one such Seller, it is wise to disclose specifics only *after* you have a firm and binding deal. At that time, you can ask your Realtor to advise the Buyer's Realtor of the specifics and the price you are seeking. If the Buyer has any interest, he can arrange to see the items, and make a decision before completion date.

The danger in revealing your willingness too early, is that the interested Buyer may simply write those items as ***inclusions*** in his offer, in an attempt to make them part of the deal. You however, want to realize some incremental value for these items.

REMEMBER..... Don't complicate the sale of your home! Selling your *home* is your priority. Worry about selling surplus chattels, only *after* your home sale is firm.

5. SIGNATURES AND THE PROPERTY CONDITION DISCLOSURE

At the same time you sign the Listing Agreement, you will be asked to complete and sign, a **"Property Condition Disclosure"** document. As the name implies, this requires you, to your best ability, to *truthfully answer a series of questions regarding the condition of your home.*

Your Realtor will be glad to explain exactly what each question means. Respond honestly, and to the best of your knowledge. A Buyer is *legally entitled* to rely on your answers.

If you take liberties with your responses, the consequences may result in the loss of a sale, once the Buyer's Inspector reveals that your answers were blatantly incorrect. Perhaps even worse, major misinformation could result in *legal action* by the Buyer, even after he purchases your house.

REMEMBER..... In order for a Listing Agreement to be legal and binding, it must be signed by *all registered owners* of the property being sold. Similarly, all registered owners must sign any counter-offer, or acceptance, as it occurs.

You and your Realtor finally sign the Listing Agreement. You also sign the Property Condition Disclosure document at the same time.

With your signing of the Listing Agreement, you will have consummated what you hope will be an effective *partnership* with your Realtor, leading to the successful sale of your home!

I use the term "*partnership*" very deliberately. Your responsibilities are significant, and will become an integral part of your Realtor's efforts and success.

REMEMBER ..... For optimum success in selling, the homeowner *must* remain actively involved in a constructive and supportive partnership with his Realtor.

CHAPTER FIVE

YOUR RESPONSIBILITIES

Now that your home is *listed for sale*, **you must ensure that you fulfill a number of key responsibilities:**

- Preparation for Sale
- Home Staging
- Readiness for Showings
- Open House Arrangements
- Contact Availability

Let's examine each of these:

1. PREPARATION FOR SALE

As suggested earlier, you, hopefully, will have remedied significant repair or maintenance issues which had existed before listing. If not, fix them now – *fast!* You don't want a potential Buyer coming to see your house, only to notice a missing down-pipe or a torn screen door as soon as he steps out of his car!

2. STAGING YOUR HOME

This really is part of the preparation process. Generally, it should not cost you much money, nor take very much time.

To create a ***positive first impression***, start with the issues of ***street appeal*** and other exterior elements which immediately draw the eye.

Spend a day or two in your garden, dressing it up. Keep the grass cut and fertilized, edges trimmed, and gardens groomed, to help showcase your home. If necessary, plant a few extra shrubs or flowers, or power-wash your sidewalks and driveway. Your front garden will create one of the first impressions a potential Buyer forms, on arrival in your driveway.

Tidy your garage, tool shed, or other exterior storage areas. Make your garbage cans as neat, and as invisible, as possible. Clean your patios, decks, and your pool and spa, if you have them.

Inside your home, keep it "showing ready," in as spotless a condition as possible, even if you have to hire a cleaning service to come in weekly or bi-weekly, for the duration of your listing.

REMEMBER..... Showings can occur unexpectedly, and on extremely short notice.

It is not unknown for a Realtor and his client to drive by your home, pull over, call your Realtor, and ask if an immediate showing is possible!

Ask your Realtor what else you can do to best *present* your home for viewings. He will give you objective suggestions.

In many communities, relatively inexpensive services exist, whereby you can retain a *home staging specialist* to advise you, usually for a well-spent few hundred dollars.

Much of the advice you receive will likely focus on removing an excess of collectibles, even perhaps, some furniture pieces. The objective is to eliminate a cluttered feel. This includes jam-packed cupboards and closets.

The more spacious, bright and airy your home appears to be, the more welcoming and appealing it will be to a potential Buyer. It certainly is not necessary to go overboard, and end up with your home looking somewhat sterile and impersonal. You want to achieve a balance between lived-in and comfortable, versus cluttered and messy.

Carefully box, label, and store excess items in your attic or basement. If you don't have the space, rent a storage locker for a few months. Look upon this as an early stage in the sorting and packing process, which you will eventually have to undertake anyway!

Some Buyers suffer from allergies to animals. You do not want to eliminate this segment of the population from the ranks of your potential Buyers. If you have pets, take extra care to shampoo carpets, and to deodorize and sanitize your home. Touch up scratch marks on walls and doors.

Even if the successful staging of your home costs $500 because you retained outside expertise, view this expenditure as a very small investment. Considering that you are trying to sell an asset worth hundreds of thousands of dollars, it is well worth it.

You are very likely to recover any such investment, many times over, through achieving an earlier sale, a better price, or even both.

> **REMEMBER..... Staging your home so it can be shown to best advantage is important, and can produce a huge return on your effort.**

It is not a complicated exercise. It often can be accomplished in a matter of days and mostly by yourself.

The key is to listen to your Realtor and others who can view your home objectively.

Their advice will help you focus on what can, and should, be done to add to your home's appeal.

3. STANDING BY FOR SHOWINGS

Your Realtor will usually, but not always, be able to give you reasonable notice if someone wishes to view your home. It's very difficult for him to influence the timing of showings, unless his own client-Buyer is involved.

Ideally, let your Realtor know that you are prepared to accommodate most showings, *even on very short notice.* Occasionally, if you are in the midst of a special event such as a family birthday party, when someone wants to view your home, you may have to explain and try to schedule another appointment time.

> **REMEMBER..... The more potential Buyers who view your home, the greater the chance of an offer!**

It pays to be as flexible as possible. This, of course, means that you and your family must keep your home in *"showing-ready"* condition, understandably not the easiest thing to do for a family with children, a dog and a hectic schedule! But, with the stakes so high, it is definitely worth the extra effort.

4. OPEN HOUSES

There are two types of open houses: one for **Realtors** to walk through and preview your home, shortly after it is listed; and the other, most often held on a Saturday or Sunday, for the **general public.**

It is very important that your Realtor set up a **"Realtor Open"** as soon as possible after listing your home for sale, and that you be receptive to it. You want as many other Realtors as possible to become familiar with your home. This will increase the chance that they will bring one of their clients through on a showing.

Ask your Realtor if it's a good idea for you to prepare snacks and coffee for the Realtors. They will appreciate it, and may linger longer in your home, which is to *your* benefit as a Seller.

Regular **open houses for the public** are to be encouraged. Open houses are an important component of the marketing plan. Yes, you can expect many neighbours, but remember, they may be your best advocates with friends and acquaintances. Some "Looky Lou's" will visit, but they too may help to spread the word. Most important is that you will also attract potential Buyers.

Open houses provide an opportunity for other Realtors to send their clients through your home without having to first make a specific appointment. They will usually alert your Realtor ahead of time, that they are sending one of their clients to your open house. This eliminates potential issues regarding their commission eligibility, should *their* client end up buying your home as a result of an initial viewing at your open house, even if unaccompanied by his Realtor.

For an open house to be truly successful, it should be advertised ahead of time by your Realtor. This is particularly important if you are located in a private cul-de-sac, or other hard-to-find area which has few drive-by opportunities.

At the time of listing, clarify your Realtor's intentions with respect to frequency of open houses, as well as his obligation to advertise them.

REMEMBER..... The more open houses, the better. Open houses attract potential Buyer traffic through your home!

5. CONTACT AVAILABILITY

During the entire time period of your listing, you must ensure that your Realtor can reach you at all times, especially if you will be out of town.

Provide your Realtor with all necessary phone numbers, as well as your e-mail address, if you have one. This is vital not only for notification of showings but also, should your Realtor receive an offer, he must be able to contact you quickly. You certainly don't want to lose a Buyer simply because you were unavailable to your Realtor.

For showings, consider this. At the time of listing, give your Realtor standing authority to permit showings, if he cannot reach you for specific verbal permission in a reasonable period of time. Request that he leave a message for you, as to the date and time of the showing he has approved. You can then accommodate yourself to the arrangement, once you learn about it. This approach is designed to ensure that you do not miss out on any showings.

Most Realtors will place on your home, a secure, computerized *lock box* containing your house key. This provides easy access for Realtors with approval to show your home. The box contains a chip which automatically records the Realtor's access code, and the date and time of entry, making this a very safe, secure and convenient arrangement.

Keep in mind that, even if your home is well-priced, it may take fifteen or more showings to potential Buyers before an offer is forthcoming.

REMEMBER...... Consider every showing, and every open house, as a valuable step along the path to selling your home.

Every potential Buyer who views your home brings you one step closer to a successful sale.

Treat each showing as if the party viewing your home *will* be making an offer. *It just may be the one to do so!*

....

If you work with your Realtor to implement all of the above, you will have laid a strong foundation for an effective partnership with him, and you will have significantly increased your odds of selling.

CHAPTER SIX

THE MARKETING PROCESS

Now the real work begins for the Realtor you have hired. You should understand what he needs to do, and support him in any way you can. Feel free to ask him questions if you are confused about any part of the process as it unfolds.

Remember however, that you have hired your Realtor to apply *his* expertise in achieving the successful sale of your home.

Be supportive of his strategy, as long as it is broadly consistent with his undertakings to you in his original proposal, and in your discussions at the time of listing.

Immediately after you sign the Listing Agreement, your Realtor will submit it to the local **Real Estate Board**. In some areas, he will load the listing and pictures directly into the local Board's system. This process will ensure that your listing appears immediately on both the Board's "in-house" information websites, which are available to all Realtors, and on a separate site for access by the general public.

Your Realtor will also launch his **marketing program** which will include:

- Open Houses
- Signage
- Floor Plans
- Photographs
- Website
- Brochure
- Advertising

Open houses have been discussed in some detail in the previous chapter. Let's now deal with the other elements of an effective marketing program:

1. SIGNAGE

Up goes the big *"For Sale"* sign in front of your home, for all your neighbours and the drive-by world to see!

Don't be one of the few Sellers who absolutely refuses to have a sign on his lawn. You *want* the neighbours and as many others as possible, to know about your home's availability. The more exposure your home has, the greater the chance of a potential Buyer wanting to see it.

I sold quite a number of homes strictly as a result of an initial drive-by interest which developed into an offer.

2. FLOOR PLANS

Most Realtors today will want to hire a *space-measuring company* to visit your home shortly after listing, to take *precise* measurements. They will draw up detailed floor plans for your Realtor's brochure. This takes a few hours, but you need not leave your home while it is being done. The cost is covered by your Realtor.

3. PHOTOGRAPHS

For his brochure and website, your Realtor will either personally take numerous photographs of both the interior and exterior of your home, or he will arrange for a professional photographer to do so. The time involved may be several hours, depending on the size of your home, with any cost again assumed by your Realtor.

4. WEBSITE

In addition to the previously-mentioned MLS website, most successful Realtors today will have their own comprehensive website which provides extensive exposure to potential Buyers, not only locally, but also from other communities, both national and international.

Your home should be prominently featured and described, with inclusion of some of the best photographs, as well as key listing information.

It's surprising how many hits these websites receive. Equally impressive is the number of actual showings and offers that result. The vast majority of potential Buyers find MLS and Realtor websites to be an invaluable starting point for their search.

5. BROCHURE

Most top Realtors will create a comprehensive and attractive brochure on your home, to be given to each potential Buyer who visits either during an open house, or by appointment. It is also easily mailed or couriered world-wide to parties who have expressed interest in your property.

An effective brochure will be extremely eye-catching, with colour photos, accurate floor plans, and all relevant information about both your home and your property. It will highlight *special* features pertaining to your home and neighbourhood.

The objective is to provide for the potential Buyer, a visual, detailed reminder of all memorable aspects of your home, once he returns home, head spinning, after viewing five or six other homes.

Your Realtor will want *your* home to stand out for the potential Buyer, possibly prompting him to ask for a second, more detailed viewing.

It is almost always necessary for a prospective Buyer to view a home *at least twice* before writing an actual offer. An exceptional brochure can help trigger that second viewing, and bring you a very important step closer to an offer.

6. ADVERTISING

Effective and *regular* advertising by your Realtor is an important means of promoting your home, and the open houses he periodically schedules.

The results of a recent particularly interesting study demonstrated that homes sell:

- 15% faster than average, if the word "*beautiful*" is used in ads;
- 20% faster than average, if "*attractive landscaping*" is mentioned;
- 12% faster, if "*move-in*" condition is included in the ads.

REMEMBER..... *Words* themselves do not lead to sales but they do draw attention, which in turn attracts more showings; *and,* if the description is accurate, they help to attract more offers.

You will want your Realtor to use such descriptions, but *only* if they are truly accurate. The potential Buyer and his Realtor will be less than impressed when viewing your home, if the description that drew them to look at it, was clearly not in keeping with reality!

The same study also determined that describing a home as *"vacant"* or a *"must see"* had no discernible impact. On the other hand, referring to it as a *"rental"* property delayed the sale by 60% over the average listing, possibly because it created the perception of a home that has been well-used, if not abused.

This study was independently undertaken by Paul Anglin, a Real Estate Professor at the University of Guelph, Ontario. The study sample involved 20,000 listings over a three-year period, from information provided by the Windsor-Essex County Real Estate Board.

Again, always be mindful that your Realtor is a *professional* whom you have hired. He is however, a busy person, and not infallible. He will always appreciate your noticing any *factual* errors in any of his marketing tools, so that he can correct them.

As long as you do not go overboard, your Realtor should be willing to listen, and to respond to your questions or constructive suggestions – after all, *you* are paying the bill!

The above elements of the marketing plan are not meant to be exhaustive. They certainly should however, be key and visible parts of your Realtor's plan.

CHAPTER SEVEN

MARKET REACTION

1. THE FIRST TWO WEEKS

In a very strong Seller's Market, you might experience a rush of showings immediately that your Listing appears on the Multiple Listing Service (MLS). *That, however exciting and welcome, would be quite unusual.*

It is more likely that any real activity, with respect to showings, would not commence for some days. It takes time for your Realtor to fully launch his marketing plan, including setting up the Realtor open, as well as your first public open house.

Scheduling advertisements, photographs, floor plans, and brochure preparation all take time. This means that your home will not be fully exposed to the market for a week to ten days. Sometimes a listing agreement will be post-dated by a week or two to allow the extra time for these necessary preparations.

This slight delay gives you a chance to complete your own sale preparations, including your staging, to ensure that your home is in its best possible viewing condition, by the time the actual *traffic* of potential Buyers begins.

2. FREQUENCY OF SHOWINGS

Once your home is fully exposed to the market, the showings should begin. If your home is properly priced, there should be quite a number of them.

After thirty days or so, this initial volume of viewings will probably diminish because the benefit of your "new to the market" exposure has worn off. You should however, continue to experience steady interest, of at least one or two showings a week, unless yours is a high-end house where showing frequency will tend to be much lower.

Open houses, and on-going advertising, are key tools the Realtor will continue to employ, to ensure that your home remains front and centre in the market.

There is no magic number of showings which will guarantee you an offer. The average will vary greatly with the type of market into which you are selling. If you are lucky, and have listed during a strong Seller's Market, you might experience two or three quick showings, and even receive simultaneous multiple offers. *You should be so lucky!*

In a more Balanced Market, don't become discouraged even if you have had ten showings, with no sign yet of an offer.

The key is whether or not showings are steadily occurring!

Your house can not be the best fit for all potential Buyers. Although individuals may react positively to your home, they may indeed go on to find another home which better meets their needs.

It is a matter of simple probabilities:

The more people who view your home, the greater your chance of an offer!

The Realtor's focus therefore, should always be to create traffic through your home.

During my years in the real estate field, I calculated that my average listing needed fifteen showings before an offer was received. This was during periods of a generally Balanced, to modest Seller's market. Don't fixate on that figure however, because during that time some of my listings sold after one showing, and others took thirty or more!

3. REALTOR FEEDBACK

Throughout the process of showings and open houses, a good Realtor will always provide feedback as best he can, for each event. He will attempt to communicate with each Realtor who requested a showing, ask for feedback, and pass that information on to you.

Recognize that he will be more successful with some Realtors than with others, but it is always worth the effort. Both you and your Realtor will gain at least some indication of the market's reaction to your home.

Feedback after his open houses is much easier for your Realtor to provide. The information will be much more precise, since he will have personally seen and heard the reactions of the visiting public.

You need not play telephone tag with your Realtor. It is sufficient that he leave a message on your answering machine, or send you an e-mail or text message.

This combined feedback will provide valuable input for both of you as, over time, you assess the effectiveness of the marketing effort, and the appropriateness of your pricing.

If your Realtor does not provide routine feedback, ask him to do so.

4. EARLY POSITIVE SIGNALS

Within the first thirty days, you and your Realtor will have developed a good *feel* for how the market is responding to your listing.

Hopefully, the signals you are receiving are *positive*. If so, the following will likely exist:

- **Positive response and feedback, from Realtors attending the Realtors' Open.**
- **A reasonably steady stream of showings by both your, and other Realtors.**

  Although it's difficult to determine what constitutes a desirable number, keep in mind that the **greatest number of showings will occur during the first four to six weeks of a new listing,** precisely because it *is* new! As the listing matures, the showings frequency will fall off.
- **A substantial number of visitors at your open houses, especially during the first few opens.**

  Again, it's difficult to quantify a good turnout versus a poor one, but your Realtor will have a good idea. If your house is not centrally located, a turnout of six or eight may be very good, unless they are all your relatives!

  Each party attending an open house in your more rural or remote neighbourhood, had to *first* locate your home, and took the trouble to do so. This suggests that such visitors are more likely to be serious Buyers, and not just cruising around for something to do.

In a high-traffic area where drive-bys can stop on a whim, twenty visitors to your open house may not have the same potential, as the half dozen visiting a quieter, less central location.

- **The length of time which potential Buyers spend in your home.**

  It is a very good sign if some people linger at your open house, or better still, arrange to return a few days later, for another look. Second showings, whether arranged by other Realtors, or by yours, are very positive indicators. Even without an offer, such activity demonstrates that your home appears to be priced reasonably enough to attract significant interest.

  If the signals are indeed positive, continued effective marketing by your Realtor, and maximum cooperation from you, should eventually lead to an offer.

Keep in mind, it is not unusual to take 60 to 120 days to attract an offer, even on a well-priced house. 180 days would not be unusual for a high-end house. Be patient!

REMEMBER..... Price is a key factor, but it is *only one* of several considerations in a Buyer's decision to make an offer on your home.

The home must meet *all* the key needs of the Buyer. It may take some time to find the right fit. This again emphasizes the importance of **maximum exposure and multiple showings of your home!**

5. EARLY NEGATIVE SIGNALS

If, in the first thirty days, negative signals predominate, sit down with your Realtor to review strategy.

Negative signals would include few showings, poor turnout and response at open houses, and the obvious, lukewarm reaction of other Realtors.

What needs to change?

Again, price is only one factor. Is the marketing plan unfolding as promised? Can the advertising frequency be increased, broadened or otherwise improved? These questions should be carefully considered, as importantly as price.

A very *low frequency of showings* will often occur when the Seller has insisted on a higher listing price than recommended, or when the Realtor has *"bought"* the listing by suggesting a very high listing price, which the Sellers were only too delighted to hear!

REMEMBER..... Unrealistic pricing does you no favours.

It causes you to miss out on that normal surge of showings which should accompany the introduction of a well-priced home to the market. It delays your sale, and may ultimately net you a lower price than you would have achieved, had you priced your home appropriately in the first place.

6. PRICE ADJUSTMENT?

If your Realtor has indeed followed an aggressive marketing plan, and has satisfied you that price is the main problem, work with him to arrive at an adjusted price.

This first price adjustment is extremely critical because, unless you are in a drastically changing market, it should be the *only* adjustment you need to make.

Why?

If I, as either a Realtor or potential Buyer, were to see a listing that has had two, three or even more price adjustments, I would have the perception (rightly or wrongly) that the Seller must be getting desperate to sell, or that the house has significant problems.

Should a Buyer like the home, he will be tempted to make a *lowball* offer, at a greater discount than he would have offered before the price started trending downward. It is human nature to bargain-hunt. The multiple price reductions have signalled that the Seller may be receptive to *any* offer.

Such negative market perceptions are best avoided. Generally, if one or two price adjustments do not result in a sale, you may be better served to let the listing expire.

You can then re-list at some later date, perhaps with a change of Realtors, if you perceive that your current Realtor contributed to your pricing problems, or if he did not execute the marketing plan well.

The Seller of course, does not always have the luxury of waiting, particularly in instances of out-of-town relocation, or family hardship. But if you can, consider a pause in the sale effort.

Again, this emphasizes the importance of selecting the ***right*** *Realtor at the outset, and setting the initial price reasonably close to the* ***real*** *market value.*

CHAPTER EIGHT

THE OFFER!

Finally! After much preparation, listing, showings, open houses and anxiety, you receive a call from your Realtor. **An offer is coming!**

An exciting time now awaits you. Again, learn what to expect, and how to handle to your best advantage, *your* role in the unfolding process.

In most cases, your offer will come through another Realtor. He may wish to personally present it to you and your Realtor. In other instances, the Realtor will fax, or otherwise convey, the offer to your Realtor, thus leaving it to him to present it to you.

Should the Realtor with the offer present it *in person*, conduct yourself very carefully! Do not tip your hand to indicate whether you are happy or unhappy with what you hear. By all means ask clarifying questions so everything is clear, but put on your best *poker face*. Otherwise you are at risk of undermining your Realtor's subsequent bargaining power on your behalf.

REMEMBER..... Your Realtor is paid by you, and indeed obligated, to achieve the best possible price for you without losing the deal.

He is far better able to do so with his extensive experience, than you are with your untutored comments or facial expressions!

If you are indeed fortunate, and the offer comes to you from one of *your* Realtor's other clients, you will be asked by him, to sign a *"Limited Dual Agency Agreement"*. This is an acknowledgement that you accept his representing both the Buyer and you, the Seller, in this particular transaction. The Buyer will be required to sign the same acknowledgement. *This topic is further discussed under "Agency Relationships" in Part IV.*

Your Realtor has accepted in this instance, a particularly tricky responsibility. He has a clear obligation to represent fairly, the interests of both the Buyer *and* the Seller. While this is akin to suggesting that he walk on water, most Realtors will do their very best to act professionally toward both parties.

You might well wonder how your Realtor can possibly be working to get *you* the best deal, in those instances when he represents both Buyer and Seller! And you are right to wonder. His responsibility in such cases is to obtain a fair deal for *each* of his clients. In negotiations, he *must not* reveal either the Buyer's or the Seller's bottom-line position to the other party. If he were to do so, he would at best, be acting unprofessionally.

There is no doubt that, as a Seller, you are losing a bit of an edge in the bargaining process; so too is the Buyer. Hopefully the effect balances out! At least you now have what you have worked so hard toward – an offer!

The process usually works very well. In fact, it is often easier to arrive at a middle ground when only one, rather than two, Realtors is acting as intermediary. There are plusses and minuses to each situation.

I personally completed about fifty such transactions. The deal was always achieved in a manner wherein both parties and I were comfortable with both the process, and the outcome.

....

For every offer, there are key elements with which the Seller must be thoroughly familiar, if he is to respond to best advantage. In summary, they are:

- Understanding the Offer
- Price
- Deposit
- Inclusions
- Dates
- Conditions of Offer
- Time Frames for Acceptance
- Responding to the Offer

Let's deal with each individually:

1. UNDERSTANDING THE OFFER

Before you can intelligently respond to an offer, you must thoroughly understand it. First, let's understand the *legal* status of both an offer and your reply.

The Buyer's offer represents his willingness to enter into a **Contract of Purchase and Sale** on your home, on the exact terms and conditions set out in his offer.

Note that this Contract of Purchase and Sale, while legally binding and enforceable *once properly executed*, is only an ***Interim Agreement***. It is this Interim Agreement that your Lawyer or Notary will use as the basis for drafting the *final* documents which are signed by both parties to the transaction, just before completion date.

Only when *all* owners on title have signed acceptance of an offer, *without any changes*, do both parties have a legally binding contract.

It would be most unusual for a Seller to sign the contract precisely as written in the initial offer.

Unless you are really desperate to sell, or the offer is truly outstanding in all respects, it is normal to *counter-offer*. Even with a fully acceptable price, it is likely that details such as dates and inclusions may require some revision to suit both parties.

It is important however, that your *counter-offer* be well thought out, and above all, reasonable.

If you should somehow offend the potential Buyer, or ignore items that are clearly important to him, he may simply tell his Realtor to forget your house, and to show him other properties. You are unlikely to hear again from that particular Buyer, or his Realtor.

If *your* Realtor is attentive, he may have picked up on signals from the offering Realtor, and will be able to help tune you in to what is particularly important to the potential Buyer. Even without this added insight, he will be able to counsel you on a reasonable counter-offer.

Carefully evaluate that advice before deciding on a formal response. Your Realtor will then draft the document to ensure that it is in correct legal form.

REMEMBER..... It is in your best interest to be reasonable when countering!

Every time you counter-offer, you pass control back to the Buyer. Only he can decide whether to respond further, or to walk away. *You always want to hear back from the Buyer!*

2. PRICE

Obviously, your eyes will gravitate first to the *dollar amount* being offered. For the Seller, this is the single-most important element of an offer.

Do not be offended by any offer! It is rare indeed, for a Buyer to offer your exact asking price. Depending on the type of market in which you are selling, his initial offer may be 10%, or even 15%, below your asking price.

Remember too, our "bargain hunter" who may offer a deeply discounted price, on the chance that yours is a "distress sale". Even he, if he likes your house enough, may increase his price significantly in subsequent counter-offers.

Some cultures believe strongly in an extended bargaining process, to satisfy themselves that they did not pay more than the minimum a Seller is willing to accept. They are not trying to offend, but rather, consider it the appropriate procedure in making such a major expenditure.

A "lowball" price offer could signal one of a number of possibilities:

- the Buyer truly believes your asking price is much too high;
- the Buyer is testing to see if you are desperate;
- the Buyer is bargain-hunting, and will buy only at bargain prices;
- the Buyer truly believes that this is the correct negotiating style.

Regardless, the Buyer *is* interested in your home. Treat his offer very seriously.

3. DEPOSIT

Every offer will specify a dollar amount of deposit, usually to be tendered on acceptance of the contract, and paid into the Realtor's *Trust Account.* If subsequently, any conditions of the offer are not removed, and the contract is thereby voided, the deposit must be returned, in full, to the Buyer.

Once a contract becomes firm and binding on both parties, the presence of a substantial deposit in a trust account represents significant protection for the Seller. Failure to complete by a Buyer leaves the deposit sum available, potentially to be applied against any damages that may legally flow from such failure.

REMEMBER..... The amount of deposit is very important to a Seller.

Five to ten percent of the agreed purchase price is a reasonable target to aim for. A lesser deposit may be appropriate in specific circumstances, rather than lose a deal. Again, your experienced Realtor will be able to provide sound advice with respect to the deposit amount.

4. INCLUSIONS

The offer will always specify the items (chattels and/or fixtures) the Buyer wants included in the purchase.

Hopefully, both he and his Realtor had already noted in the listing information, *your* preferences in this regard. If the Buyer has accepted for example, your wish to take your appliances with you, then this will not be an issue in the ensuing negotiations. On the other hand, if he does want them, it can become a negotiating point.

Clearly, there exists a price level at which you would be pleased to leave them! Look beyond a particular item. Rather, see how it fits in with the rest of the offer, and with your overall end-result expectations.

5. COMPLETION, POSSESSION, AND ADJUSTMENT DATES

Every offer will always contain these three dates.

The **completion date** is the date on which the Buyer is willing to complete the financial part of the transaction; namely, pay you, via your Lawyer or Notary Public, the agreed-upon sum of money.

The **possession date** is the date when he wishes to occupy his new home. This could vary from the date you, the Seller, receive payment through your Lawyer or Notary, to a day or two later. **Regardless of the circumstances, confirmation of payment must *always* precede possession.**

The **adjustment date** is the date up to which, the Seller pays property taxes and utilities, and from which, the Buyer begins paying them. It will usually fall on either the completion date, or more likely, the possession date.

If the offered dates meet your needs, and you can accept them, they will not be an issue.

On the other hand, if the dates present a major problem for you, it may be a good idea, before putting pen to paper in a series of counter-offers, that your Realtor discuss with the offering Realtor, what flexibility exists on the Buyer's part, and convey where your problem and flexibility lie.

It is rare to lose a deal on a disagreement over dates. Usually these can be sorted out amicably.If the dates are critical to a Buyer because for example, he is driven by an obligation to vacate his current residence, do your best to be flexible. Recognize that a Buyer may have a more pressing need for the offered dates, than you, as a Seller, will have for changing them.

REMEMBER..... Always consider the problem you have with a *detail* in the offer, in the context of the *total* offer.

At the right price, you are better served to move out, and stay in a hotel for a month if you have to – or even better, stay with relatives for free, or take a vacation!

6. CONDITIONS OF OFFER

Almost every offer to purchase will contain one or more conditions which must be met, *to the satisfaction of the Buyer*, before he is willing to be bound by his offer.

Among many possibilities, the most frequent conditions are:

- **Subject to Financing; and**
- **Subject to Inspection.**

The reality is that, until the condition, or conditions are satisfied, the Buyer can back out of his offer, simply by failing to remove any one of his conditions, by the date and time set out in the contract.

The following illustrates typical wording of the above two conditions:

a) *"Subject to the purchaser arranging, on or before June 15, 2007, a conventional mortgage in the amount of $250,000 with an interest rate not exceeding 6% per annum, calculated semi-annually, and with a 25-year amortization. This condition is for the sole benefit of the purchaser."*

b) *"Subject to the purchaser being satisfied with the results of an independent inspection, arranged and paid for by the purchaser, on or before June 18, 2007. This condition is for the sole benefit of the purchaser."*

The first condition, **Subject to Financing,** is entirely reasonable, in that the Buyer must be 100% certain that his financial institution will advance him the funds he requires to complete the transaction, as agreed in the contract.

The second condition, **Subject to Inspection**, is almost always recommended by the Buyer's Realtor and generally, should be included in the offer. It is intended to ensure that there are no *major* hidden surprises if the Buyer proceeds with the purchase.

Consider for example, roof condition as a major, possible issue. The roof may look satisfactory to the untrained eye. A professional inspection however, may indicate that it will likely need replacement within two to five years. Although the purchaser may well accept such news and proceed with the purchase, *he wants the right* to make such a decision, to renegotiate price, or to walk away from the deal.

Your Realtor will advise you on what constitutes reasonable or unreasonable conditions. However, the aforementioned are relatively standard. Your Realtor will also want to ensure that the time period specified for the satisfaction of all conditions is reasonable.

In the two examples above, you can expect the time frame to be five to ten working days. It should rarely be more, because the Buyer is effectively tying up your ability to accept another offer during this period, without any firm assurance that he will remove his conditions, and hence commit to complete the transaction.

The inclusion of the words ***"for the sole benefit of the purchaser"*** permits the Buyer the sole discretion to perform, or not perform, the specified action, yet still remove the condition.

For example, he may on second thought, decide that his own thorough inspection of the house makes hiring a professional Inspector unnecessary. *He* can then choose to forego the inspection. If he does remove that specific condition, you, the Seller cannot object nor escape the contract, just because the Buyer did not carry through on an Inspection.

The same is true of the financing condition. After inclusion of this condition, a generous relative perhaps offers to provide the necessary funds. As a result, the Buyer no longer requires either a mortgage or the financing condition.

You really don't care under what circumstances the Buyer removes his conditions, as long as he does so, and the contract becomes firm and binding on both parties.

....

You, the Seller, may occasionally wish to accept an offer with *a condition of your own*. Here's the most common example:

"Subject to the Seller firming up the purchase of a replacement home on terms satisfactory to him, on or before (48 to 72 hours from the date of offer). This condition is for the sole benefit of the Seller."

Again, your Realtor will advise you whether a specific condition which you wish to add is reasonable, given the total circumstances set out in the offer.

REMEMBER..... The fewer roadblocks you throw up before the Buyer, the better your chances of reaching agreement.

Hopefully you have done sufficient homework *before listing* to avoid the need for your own conditions. Under a few rare circumstances however, they may be appropriate and even advisable.

Be very cautious in your consideration of an offer with a "Subject to Sale" condition. This arises when a potential Buyer really likes your home, and wants to buy it, but can not afford to, or does not want to complete the purchase until he has a firm sale on his current home.

In this case the Buyer's condition may read something like:

> *"Subject to the purchaser concluding an unconditional contract for the sale of his home located at 123 Shady Lane, Sarnia, on or before August 31, 2007. This condition is for the sole benefit of the purchaser."*

The date inserted in this case will often be 60 to 90 days in the future. Usually there will be a coincident commitment to remove all other conditions, such as inspection and financing, within the next week to ten days, leaving only the **"Subject to Sale"**condition outstanding.

Do not reject such a condition out of hand, but be aware of the pros and cons. If you *were* to consider accepting, your Realtor will advise you to respond with your own protective condition, along these lines:

> *"Subject to the Seller giving the purchaser 48 hours' notice in which to remove the subject to sale condition, should the Seller receive another acceptable offer in the intervening period. This condition is for the sole benefit of the Seller."*

The *downside* of accepting a **"Subject to Sale"** condition, even with the outlined protection for the Seller, may be significant. Consider this:

- Your Realtor may pull back, more than you would like, from his aggressive marketing effort, because he believes you have a probable deal on the table.
- In the real estate community, it is not unusual for word to get around that you have accepted a **"Subject to Sale"** deal. If they do become aware of the existence of a "subject" agreement, Realtors will be less willing to consider showing your home because it may well be a waste of their time. They know that should they end up writing an acceptable offer, you are contractually obliged to give the required notice to the original Buyer. He *may* then choose to remove his subject-to-sale condition and firm up his deal. If he does so, the second potential Buyer is left with no possible agreement.
- You have absolutely no control over the saleability of the Buyer's home. It may be overpriced or, for any number of other reasons, hard to sell.

- Two or three months after accepting a **"Subject to Sale"** offer, you could find yourself still without a firm deal. You and your Realtor would then have to somehow rekindle market interest – no easy feat after your home has been on offer for three or four months!

If you have considered these potential risks, and decide to accept this condition, you would normally do so at a *higher* price than you would contemplate without such a condition. It is fairly normal for **"Subject to Sale"** contracts to be written *at*, or *very close to*, asking price, to compensate for some of the risk that the Seller is accepting.

7. TIME FRAMES FOR ACCEPTANCE

It is normal and indeed, good business practice, for the offer to include a specified date and time for acceptance.

Typically, the Buyer's Realtor will suggest a length of time, of no less than four hours, but rarely more than 24 hours. This forces you, the Seller, to be efficient in analyzing the offer, and to be prompt in responding.

If you respond *even one minute* past the indicated deadline, the offer has legally lapsed.

The only ways it can be resurrected are:

- *Both* Buyer and Seller *each* initial a change to the date and time of acceptance;

or

- The Buyer submits a new offer.

Effectively, by not replying within the time frame specified in the offer, you have returned control of the situation to the Buyer.

This is *not* a good idea, so work hard with your Realtor to meet the deadline. The process works both ways. If *you* make a counter-offer, you also will specify a time frame for the Buyer's acceptance.

These deadlines are fair to both parties, and ensure that the process continues to move forward, to a reasonably quick conclusion.

8. RESPONDING TO THE OFFER

After thoroughly reviewing the offer with your Realtor, ensuring that you, and all others on title, understand exactly what is being offered, your Realtor will assist you in framing a response, all within the specified time frame.

Never feel so offended by any written offer, that you decide to not reply, thereby letting it lapse!

Recall how hard you and your Realtor have worked to get this offer! It would be ridiculous to let it lapse without testing sufficiently to see if the offered terms can be moved toward your minimum requirements. Neither you nor your Realtor can be certain that the Buyer will not improve his initial offer, even drastically.

I have been in situations when an initial offer, almost 15% below the listing price, ended up within a fully acceptable 2%! One such negotiation took five or six offers and counter-offers, and many hours, but finally, a deal was struck, and the transaction subsequently closed successfully.

Should you ever be fortunate enough to encounter that rare instance when the initial offer meets *all* of your expectations, including price, responding to the offer is a simple exercise. First, you leap into the air shouting **"YES!"** Then you signify your acceptance by signing off on the offer.

All owners on title must signify their acceptance by signing the contract as written, after which your Realtor returns it to the Buyer's Realtor. You would then have a deal, subject to any *conditions* specified in the contract being satisfied and removed, within the time frame set out.

It is more likely however, that you will be responding with *some* modification to the offered terms.

It is important that *your Realtor*, not you, make any required modifications to the original *Agreement of Purchase and Sale* document.

It is his job to write your required changes into the contract in a manner that protects your legal interests. All you need do is initial all changes, and sign the document, indicating your acceptance of the Buyer's offer, with your changes incorporated. Then of course, it's up to the Buyer to accept, or counter-offer once again with his modifications.

Carefully consult with your Realtor on the *potential consequences* of every item or issue that you initially feel you might wish to change. Reduce this list to a minimum.

Concentrate on modifying only the most important issues!

For example, the Buyer wants your washer and dryer, which you had planned to take. Consider *not* countering on that point! It is not important enough, is worth a relatively small amount of money, and you will enjoy a new set in your next home.

Issues which can be quantified, as in this example, as equivalent dollars of value, can easily be recovered to your satisfaction if the selling price is adequate. The *more important issues* are generally price, dates, and conditions.

REMEMBER.....	**Your objective always, is to try to obtain the Buyer's acceptance of your counter-offer; *not* to cause him to walk away.**

There is little value at this point, to suggesting specific negotiating strategies, because each case will differ. Your Realtor will be best tuned in to the needs of the Buyer and his Realtor.

This is when a *superior* Realtor clearly distinguishes himself, and earns the commission you are paying him. He will rarely allow a deal to be lost.

I can recall having only three, of hundreds of deals, fall apart irretrievably, during the negotiations phase.

Usually a middle ground, acceptable to both parties, can be found. The solution may require extreme creativity, but an experienced Realtor should be able to lead the process to a successful conclusion.

At the right price, a Seller is wise to try to accommodate most elements of a Buyer's offer. Here is a rather extreme, but true, example:

One of my listings was a beautiful home, listed at what I considered to be the maximum possible price of $699,000, in a suburb of Vancouver. I had warned the owners that listing so high could delay a potential sale and that it may require a significant price reduction.

After several months of extensive effort, I finally wrote an unconditional offer from a foreign Buyer who visited one of my open houses.

I drove to the Sellers' summer cottage with the offer. I still recall my exact words:

"I have good news, but also bad news, for you both. The good news is that I have a full price, unconditional offer for your home, with completion in ten days. The bad news is that if you accept the offer, the Buyer will own everything in your home, except your underwear and personal photographs!"

My Sellers' initial reaction was shock. But after some thirty minutes of reflection and discussion, they realized that this was an exceptionally good deal.

Not only were my Sellers offered a superb price, but also, they were given the unexpected opportunity to purchase new furniture to better suit the much smaller home they planned to buy. Additionally, they were now faced with zero packing and moving costs!

For the Buyer, who planned to use the house only two or three months a year, purchasing a fully-furnished and outfitted house was extremely important. He liked the furniture and the paintings in this home, and did not have the time, nor the desire, to set about the chore of furnishing a huge house.

I am certain that this Buyer would have walked away from the deal, even at a discounted price, had the Sellers refused to include the furnishings.

My Sellers signed the contract as written, and received their full asking price!

CHAPTER NINE

THE ROAD TO ACCEPTANCE

Hopefully, after one, two, three, or even more careful exchanges, you will have a properly executed Agreement for Purchase and Sale on your home.

This is an extremely important step. However, unless you were extremely fortunate in concluding on an offer with no conditions, *you cannot yet relax.*

All conditions, both yours as Seller, and the Buyer's, must be removed within their specified time frames, before the contract becomes firm and binding on both parties.

The road to a completed sale requires that the Seller understand the next series of steps, necessary to the achievement of eventual success:

- Removal of conditions
- Inspection results
- Extension of dates
- Firm and binding agreement
- Title conveyance
- Possession

1. REMOVAL OF CONDITIONS

Yours is a key role in the successful removal of all conditions.

Ensure that you do whatever is necessary to remove *your own conditions,* if you have any, prior to the specified date and time.

Your Realtor will draft the "Subject Removal" document for signatures: yours and *all* other registered owners of your property.

Make every effort to provide all *necessary* access to your home, whether by the Buyer himself, or by various agents who are acting on his behalf. Typical examples are:

- **Access by an Appraiser on behalf of the Buyer's lending institution.**The Appraiser's purpose is to independently confirm value, prior to the Buyer receiving a firm commitment for the necessary mortgage. An appraisal usually takes only 30 minutes or so, and you need not leave your home for it.
- **Access by the Buyer's Inspector.**
  The Inspector's function is to carry out a comprehensive inspection of the physical condition of your home. The Buyer will also be present during at least the last part of the inspection. Often, his Realtor will also attend to hear the results. An inspection can take two to four hours, and usually costs *the Buyer* between $250 to $400, depending on the size of the house.

  In order that the Inspector and the Buyer can communicate freely, leave your home during the entire inspection period. Should subsequent input be required of you, any questions and your responses will be properly relayed through the Realtors.

2. INSPECTION RESULTS

Do not fear an inspection! Generally, it is a necessary step, whereby a Buyer assures himself that he understands the condition of your home, before he firmly commits to proceed with a purchase. *You would expect to do the same when **you** are buying a home.*

The Inspector will generally put his findings into proper perspective for the Buyer, explaining that **it is rare indeed, to *not* identify some flaws or deficiencies, even in a new home.** The Inspector may find, for instance, a window with a failed seal, a detail which perhaps even you had not noticed. He will document and explain all deficiencies, whether minor or significant, to the Buyer.

In the vast majority of cases, an inspection does not cause a major problem for the Buyer, and he will routinely sign off on his "inspection" condition.

Even in the few cases where unexpected major issues are identified, which could threaten the sale, there are usually mutually acceptable solutions. Should you encounter this relatively rare situation, be prepared to work with your Realtor to find a remedy which is acceptable to the Buyer.

Let's examine two *possible* worst-case examples:

a) ***The Inspector identifies that the roof, although only eleven years old, will probably need replacement within the next several years. This comes as a surprise to both the Buyer and you, the Seller, since you would normally expect a roof to last twenty years or more. A new roof may cost around $15,000. The Buyer does not feel comfortable with such a large, looming expenditure.***

In this instance, the Buyer's Realtor may contact yours, to explore avenues which may be available to satisfy both parties. Should the Buyer's Realtor fail to do so, and the deal appear to be in jeopardy, then after consulting with you, *your* Realtor should take the initiative. Often the two parties will agree to a price adjustment which is roughly equivalent to the cost of the unexpected problem.

In this particular example however, it need not be the full $15,000 replacement cost. It is reasonable for a Buyer who is purchasing an eleven-year-old house to plan to pay for a new roof within the next eight or nine years. The issue is that the expenditure will likely be needed sooner, in the next year or two. A reasonable adjustment to the selling price in this case could be in the range of $5,000 to $7,000.

You may shudder at such a prospect. However, if you lose this Buyer, the same issue will likely emerge with the next offer. ***Better to resolve the issue now, and sell your home!***

b) ***Another troublesome issue that at times arises, is the condition of the septic system, in areas without a municipal sewer connection. A septic tank Inspector may find that the tank is not working properly, that the field is partially plugged or, that the tank itself needs replacing. It could even be a combination of issues.***

A septic problem is one of the most difficult to resolve because it can be very difficult to ascertain the extent of the problem, and hence the total probable cost. A Buyer is unlikely to be willing to proceed with removal of his conditions on any home with a major problem of this kind.

Recognize that *the problem will not go away* if the current deal falls through.

Furthermore, once you are aware of the problem, you are *obliged* to identify it in your **Property Condition Disclosure Document,** for a future Buyer.

This may be a case where you need to amend the contract, and commit yourself at your expense, to perform whatever repair or replacement is necessary, prior to the completion date set out in your contract.

If the Buyer accepts this solution, he will undoubtedly request both a follow-up inspection, and a comprehensive list of repairs made.

Alternatively, the Buyer may choose to accept a significant price reduction and resolve the issue himself. Again, informal discussions between the two parties, through their Realtors, can often result in a solution acceptable to both.

If, despite your best efforts, the deal does fall apart, immediately commission a reliable company to *address the problem* before another offer materializes.

Extreme examples such as the above are quite rare. I include them simply to emphasize that, with effort, solutions *can often be found*, even on major issues. Problems are best resolved with the offer at hand, rather than letting the deal collapse.

One sure way to avoid unwelcome surprises such as this, is for you, the Seller, to **commission your own independent inspection,** as part of your preparation work, *prior to listing.* You will be responsible for the cost of such an inspection, but you will also have a clear report on any deficiencies. You can then decide whether to address them before listing or, alternatively, take them into account by establishing a lower listing price, than you would otherwise have contemplated.

3. EXTENSION OF DATE FOR CONDITION REMOVAL

On occasion, the Seller will encounter a situation in which the Buyer requests a short extension of subject removal dates, in order to satisfy himself that he should proceed with the purchase.

Most often, this will arise due to extra time required to secure the necessary financing. It is generally in the Seller's interest to agree to an extension, for a *brief* period of time, usually a few days only, and rarely beyond a week. Again, your Realtor will guide you in this, and in the signing of the necessary date amendment document.

4. FIRM AND BINDING AGREEMENT

Once the Buyer has removed all of his conditions (and you, yours, if you had any) by signing off on each individual item, *both* parties are now *legally* bound by their obligation to complete the transaction.

Failure to complete on the specified completion date, can have very serious legal and financial consequences for the defaulting party.

Both parties have a *legal right* to rely on the completion occurring as committed. One, or both, may have made major commitments of their own as a direct consequence of the agreement.

For example, the Seller will often have committed, in turn, to purchase a replacement property, usually undertaking to pay for it the day after receiving the funds from the sale of his current property.

If the Buyer were then to fail to complete, he could be legally responsible for all costs incurred by the Seller as a direct consequence. This could amount to tens of thousands of dollars!

That is why Buyers must be 100% certain of their financing before firming up a house purchase.

A default on closing rarely occurs because of the *severity* of the potential consequences. Even were the Buyer to die, between the date of removal of all conditions and the date of completion, his estate would be legally obliged to honour the agreement, and complete the deal.

At times, two or three sale and purchase transactions may follow one another in a chain reaction, all completing within a day or two of each other. Imagine the liabilities which could arise if anyone in the chain were to default on his obligations!

....

A Realtor involved in a Real Estate transaction also has a major legal obligation to ensure that the agreement he has counselled his client to sign, was in good legal form, and hence enforceable.

All Realtors are required to carry liability insurance to protect themselves, *and* their clients, against major errors or omissions on the part of the Realtor.

Here again, is another reason to ***think long and hard before you decide to try to sell on your own.*** Should you choose to do so, ensure that any contract into which you enter, is *subject to legal review*, before making it firm and binding. It may complicate your dealing directly with a Buyer, but unless you are a lawyer, it would be sheer folly to do otherwise.

5. CONVEYING TITLE

If you had not pre-arranged this prior to executing a firm Contract of Purchase and Sale, you will quickly have to appoint a Lawyer or Notary to represent you.

He will convey your title to the Buyer, ensuring that this is done only *after* he holds all agreed funds (after adjustments) "In Trust", on your behalf.

6. VACANT POSSESSION

Under the contract which you have signed, you are obliged to grant the Buyer *"vacant possession"*, on the date and time specified.

The agreement also requires that you turn over the property, in substantially the same condition which existed at the time of the Buyer's last viewing. This leaves you with a number of obligations which *you* must carefully execute, before your Realtor turns the keys over to the Buyer.

Any part of the home, its fixtures, or remaining chattels, which break or cease to function during the period between contract signing and the Buyer's occupancy, must be repaired or replaced by you, the Seller, *and* at your expense. As much as possible, this should be completed prior to the occupancy date. This could include for instance, furnace or hot water tank failure, appliance breakdown, or even a broken window. Included in your obligation is the repair of damage done in the process of moving out of the house.

REMEMBER..... The Seller has a continuing obligation to maintain the home in good repair, right up to the day he turns the house over to the Buyer.

Otherwise, the new owner may have legal remedies against the Seller, even *after* the sale completes.

....

As an added *courtesy,* which the Buyer will fully appreciate, the considerate Seller will:

- Thoroughly clean the home after all furniture is removed;
- Remove garbage, and other redundant items from the garage, attic, yard, basement, or crawl space;
- Spruce up the yard by cutting the grass; complete other basic yard maintenance;
- Leave copies of appliance manuals, and equipment operating instructions in his possession;
- Label and leave any keys;
- Leave a list of helpful information such as garbage and recycling days;

and

- Any other information that *you* would like to receive from the Seller, once you buy *your* replacement home.

....

THE END RESULT....

AFTER ALL YOUR HARD WORK:

- *ALL CONDITIONS HAVE BEEN REMOVED*
- *YOU HAVE A FIRM CONTRACT*
- *YOU CAN FINALLY OPEN THAT BOTTLE OF CHAMPAGNE!*

NOW.....

YOU CAN TRULY CELEBRATE YOUR SUCCESSFUL HOME SALE, HOPEFULLY BY FIRMING UP AN OFFER, AND PURCHASING THAT PERFECT REPLACEMENT HOME YOU HAVE KEPT YOUR EYE ON THROUGHOUT YOUR SALE PROCESS.

....

Otherwise, it's time to roll up your sleeves once again, and start looking in earnest, for a replacement home.

Ideally, you will want the closing and possession dates of both transactions, your sale and your purchase, to coincide so that you can move seamlessly from one home to the next.

THE SELLER'S 10-MINUTE SUMMARY

1. Determine the state of the market before selling. Buyer's, Seller's or Balanced Market? Adjust selling strategies accordingly.
2. Planning to buy a replacement home? Do your homework before selling. Make sure that your dreams really are affordable.
3. Calculate both your projected *net* proceeds of a successful sale, and your expected cost of buying.
4. Not pressed to sell? Make sure that selling *at this time* makes sense.
5. Have a mortgage? *Before* selling, understand your present mortgage status, its portability, the incremental mortgage for which you would qualify on a replacement home, as well as the additional cost that it would represent.
6. Have a choice of timing? List your home during prime selling months.
7. Tempted to sell on your own? Fully examine the pros and cons. Generally the risks outweigh the potential benefits.
8. Retaining a Realtor? Proceed very carefully, to engage the best one possible. It costs no more to hire an exceptional Realtor than a mediocre one.
9. Negotiating the commission? Be reasonable in your expectations. "You get what you pay for".
10. Document any commission adjustment by means of a *side agreement* which does not change the commission entitlement of other Realtors.

11. **Beware the Realtor whose proposed listing price is clearly above any reasonable estimate of market value.**
12. **Do not be mesmerized by the slickness of a Realtor's listing proposal document. Scrutinize and judge the detailed content, not the glossiness.**
13. **Fully understand the contents of a Listing Agreement before you sign it.**
14. **Remain actively involved in a constructive and supportive partnership with your Realtor.**
15. **Prepare and stage your home to show it to its best advantage.**
16. **Do not diminish the saleability of your home by excluding too many fixtures.**
17. **Concentrate on selling your home. Worry about selling surplus chattels only after your home sale is firm.**
18. **Showings can occur unexpectedly and on extremely short notice. Be ready.**
19. **The more potential Buyers who view your home, the greater the chance of an offer.**
20. **The more open houses, the better. They attract potential Buyer traffic.**
21. **Consider every showing, and every open house, as a valuable step along the path to selling your home.**
22. **Treat each showing as if the party viewing your home *will* be making an offer.**
23. **Price is a key factor, but only one of several considerations in a Buyer's decision to make an offer on your home.**
24. **Unrealistic pricing does you no favours.**
25. **Your Realtor's objective is to get the best possible price and conditions on your home sale, without losing the deal.**
26. **It is in your best interest to be reasonable when countering an offer.**

27. The amount of deposit offered is important to the Seller.

28. Always consider any issue you have with an offer in the context of the *total* offer.

29. The fewer roadblocks you throw up before the Buyer, the better your chances of reaching agreement.

30. Your objective always, is to try to obtain the Buyer's acceptance of your counter-offer; not to cause him to walk away.

31. The Seller has a continuing obligation to maintain the home, in good repair, until the day he turns the house over to the Buyer.

PART III

THE BUYING PROCESS

CHAPTER TEN

THE DECISION TO PURCHASE

There are few among us who have not, on occasion, asked ourselves which is the better economic decision – to rent or to purchase?

This is an important issue to examine, whether you are contemplating the purchase of a first-time, or a replacement, home.

1. A GOOD TIME TO RENT?

There are a number of relatively specific circumstances when renting your residence should be seriously considered:

- ***You simply can not afford to buy at this time.***

Either you do not have the minimum down payment required, or you do not have sufficient household income to qualify for the necessary mortgage. This is more likely to be the case for those contemplating a first-time purchase.

If *you* find yourself in this situation, use the research that led you to this conclusion, to **lay out a personal financial plan which will allow you to qualify as soon as possible, for a purchase.** Set up a savings plan, consider taking a second part-time job, or define any other strategy that leads to your being able to enter the rank of homeowners, at the earliest possible time.

- ***You are between jobs, or very likely to be transferred by your employer to another community within the next year or two.***

If you are out of work, or looking for a career change, you may have to relocate to obtain reasonable employment. Even if you can afford to purchase without a regular salary, it may be prudent to rent until you have a clearer picture of your future.

If a work-related transfer is on the horizon, you may be well-advised to rent because *having* to sell within a year or two could trap you, for instance, in a short-term falling market, combined with the high cost of selling. Of course, if your employer is a financial institution, or other large organization which eliminates your real estate risks and costs, this would be a non-issue.

2. THE CASE FOR BUYING A HOME

In virtually all other circumstances*, purchasing a home, whether for the first time, or as a replacement for a home you have just sold, is your best long-term decision.*

a) Non-Economic Reasons

- Pride of ownership. Your own place to call "home"!
- Decision-making freedom. Ability to decorate or renovate whenever and however you desire.
- Certainty of tenure. Nobody can evict you!

b) Economic Reasons

- Increased equity value as you pay down your mortgage.
- Participation in tax-free equity growth as home values increase.
- Minimal annual cost increases, compared to rent.
- Increased credit worthiness in the eyes of Lenders.
- Ease of future upgrades to a higher-value home. Growing equity will generate the necessary increases in down payment.
- Disciplined equity growth. Paying off a mortgage is akin to a forced savings plan. You know you will make a payment each month!

A 2007 Re/Max study found that the average home in Canada has increased in value by 264% in the 25 years between 1981 and 2006.

This amounts to a surprisingly modest 5.3% annual, compounded rate of return, about twice the average rate of inflation during that period. The Toronto Stock Composite Index, on the other hand, grew by a compounded average of 7.8% during the same period.

One might question whether owning a home during this period was really the better investment – until you analyze the differences:

- The value increase in a primary residence is totally tax-free;
- The gain on the stock market or any other investment is taxable;
- The 5.3% annual gain on home values is calculated on the basis of average *full* price paid in 1981 ($80,000) compared to average *full* price ($299,000) paid in 2006. How many homeowners pay full price for an average home without borrowing some of the money?

More realistically, the typical Buyer in 1981 probably made a down payment of 25% of the purchase price, approximately $20,000, on the then-average house. After 25 years the mortgage would normally have been paid off. The real, compounded annual return on the *actual* down payment, would be 11.4%, and all of it tax free!

Some will argue that a good part of that gain comes from the payments made over the years, to liquidate the mortgage. That is correct. However, the homeowner had to live somewhere during those 25 years, so whether similar amounts were spent on rent, or on mortgage payments, really makes little difference.

With *ownership* however, tremendous equity has been created, through the combination of :

- A paid-off house;
- Market value increase;
- Strategic use of borrowing.

3. SIZE OF MORTGAGE

For the first two or three home purchases, most Buyers have little choice but to carry a large mortgage in order to purchase the home that they need or want. For them, the issue of mortgage size is somewhat academic.

There are many instances however, when Buyers *do* have a choice with respect to the size of their mortgage, or even, whether they need one at all. In these cases the following should be kept in mind:

Every mortgage payment is made with after-tax dollars.

This means that if your mortgage payment is $1000 per month and you are in a 35% marginal tax position, about *$1500 of your gross monthly income* will be required to make that payment!

Few investments are guaranteed to perform better, on an after-tax basis, than paying down the mortgage on your home.

Everyone who currently has a mortgage, or plans to have one, would be well-advised to read the book by Fraser Smith, titled "Is Your Mortgage Tax Deductible? The Smith Manoeuvre".

If you are incurring major, non-deductible interest on debt, including the interest on your mortgage, this technique can save you a huge sum of money on your interest payments, by making them tax-deductible.

REMEMBER..... Unless you have a mortgage on which the interest is tax-deductible, always try to minimize your mortgage amount. Once you have a mortgage, try to pay it down as quickly as possible!

See PART IV – MORE ON MORTGAGES for more information.

CHAPTER ELEVEN

ISSUES FOR THE BUYER

If he has just sold his home, a prospective Buyer will probably have addressed the following issues, either prior to listing, or during the listing period.

A first-time Buyer will have to start from scratch, to fully understand the issues and their answers, before proceeding too far with his search for a home.

Here again, a good Realtor can be very helpful in explaining some of the issues, including:

- The Market Environment
- Defining Your "Needs"
- Defining Your "Wants"
- Your Budget

Let's deal with these individually:

1. THE MARKET ENVIRONMENT

Equally important for the Buyer as for the Seller, **the market environment significantly affects the bargaining power of a home Buyer**.

The strategies used in the purchasing process must be aligned with the market reality if the Buyer is to achieve best possible value in his home purchase.

Review "Laying The Groundwork" Section, which discusses this topic in some detail.

Remember too, that visiting all open houses in your area is a particularly useful way to obtain a feel for the current market.

2. DEFINING YOUR "*NEEDS*"

Before a Buyer can productively focus his search, he must identify the *minimum requirements* that must be satisfied by any home he buys.

These will include:

- Neighbourhood limitations, or expectations?
- Single or multi-level? With suite?
- Residential only, or suitable for home-based business?
- Approximate overall size?
- Minimum number of bedrooms and bathrooms?
- Size and layout of kitchen?
- Carport, single or double garage?
- Size and orientation of yard?
- Proximity to schools and services?
- New home or resale?

and

- Any other features that the Buyer considers *absolutely essential.*

Don't confuse a "*needs*" list with a "*wants*" list!

Yes, you might *prefer* additional features if they are available and affordable. However, they are *not* part of your "must-have" list.

3. DEFINING YOUR "*WANTS*"

As the prospective Buyer, make a list of those features in a home, which it would be *nice to have*, but which are not absolutely essential.

Doing so ensures that these preferences are in the back of your mind as you begin the search for potentially suitable homes. This may include, among others, items such as:

- preferred type of heating system;
- existence and number of fireplaces in a home;
- preferred roof or window types.

REMEMBER.....	**Just because it may meet some, or even all, of your *"wants,"* never compromise on a basic *"need"*, when buying your home.**

If the *"need"* you are contemplating trading off was correctly defined as an absolute necessity, you are likely, sooner than later, to become extremely frustrated and unhappy after buying that home.

4. YOUR BUDGET

Whether you are a first-time Buyer, or replacing a home just sold, **know the maximum price you can afford to pay for your new home.**

To calculate your budget is not difficult. Break your effort into the following elements:

- Down Payment
- Mortgage Eligibility
- Closing Costs
- Insurance Costs
- Moving Costs
- Appraisal and Survey Costs
- Crunching the Numbers

We'll deal with each in turn:

a) Down Payment

If you have just sold a home, calculate very carefully, the actual *net* proceeds you will receive from the sale of your home, *after* all costs are deducted. *Appendix 3 will assist you with that calculation.*

If you are buying for the first time, you know precisely how much money you have saved.

As a first-time Buyer, with a large enough RRSP, current legislation allows you to *borrow* up to $20,000 from your RRSP, toward your down payment. If you are a couple, you may each borrow $20,000, assuming each account holds sufficient funds.

Keep in mind however, that you are required to repay the borrowed amount to your RRSP over the next 15 years, or face substantial tax obligations.

....

Let's assume that our Buyer, in this example, will have available to him for his next home purchase, a total of $90,000, as follows:

- $76,000 in *net* proceeds from the house he has just sold;
- $4,000 in a savings account;
- $10,000 in a Canada Savings Bond.

He is planning tentatively, to make a down payment totalling $80,000, leaving himself a $10,000 reserve for closing costs.

b) Mortgage Eligibility

By the time you, the Buyer, reach this stage, you will have obtained from your Banker, Mortgage Broker, or other Lender, an indication of the size of mortgage he would approve for you.

To obtain this vital information from a Lender, you will have provided specific details of employment, assets, present debts and associated monthly payments, and household income history. He will also check your credit rating to make sure that you have been a responsible borrower in the past.

Your Lender will use this information to make a number of calculations which, together with your credit history, will form the basis for his decision.

The two most important calculations that the Lender makes will be:

- **The Gross Debt Service Ratio (GDS)**

This is simply the percentage of your gross family income that is required to cover key payments associated with your housing. These include mortgage principal and interest payments, property taxes, and estimated utility costs.

If your requested mortgage exceeds 80% of appraised value (a high-ratio mortgage), a front-line Lender, such as a Bank, will be rigid in not allowing this ratio to exceed 32% of gross family income.

- **Total Debt Service Ratio (TDSR)**

This is a similar calculation to the GDS, except that it now includes in the calculation, all other debt payments and obligations, such as car and credit card payments.

Again, in a high-ratio mortgage situation, front-line Lenders will not advance the mortgage amount you are seeking, if doing so would see your TDSR exceed 40%.

Should your requested mortgage amount fit the definition of a conventional mortgage (less than 80% of appraised value), the Lender will use the above ratio limits only as guidelines, on which flexibility exists.

Should the payments for the requested conventional mortgage amount exceed the 32% and 40% ratios, the Lender may still approve it, if he is satisfied with respect to your credit history, capacity for repayment, other collateral offered, and very importantly, your relationship and track record historically, with that Lender.

The Lender will require verification of your gross household income. This can usually be satisfied by your last T-4 slips, or by a letter from your employer.

You can calculate these two ratios yourself, before you get too enthusiastic about that perfect house with its much larger mortgage. This will give you an early feel for how a Lender is likely to respond. Appendix 4 and Appendix 5 will allow you to easily calculate these ratios.

Keep in mind that these indications from your Lender do not, at this time, constitute a firm commitment from him. They are however, a strong signal of what you might reasonably expect by way of a future commitment.

Final approval from your Lender will occur only after you have made a conditional purchase of a home, and he has verified the home's *value through his own Appraiser.*

*The tentative nature of the Lender's initial approval is the key reason why you are wise to always include a **"Subject to Financing"** clause, in any offer which is dependent on a mortgage.*

This early indication of borrowing limits from your Lender is sufficient however, to help you calculate the maximum price you can afford to pay for a home.

....

We'll assume, in this instance, that our Lender has indicated that, given our household income and outstanding debt, we qualify for a maximum **mortgage of $300,000.**

c) Closing Costs

We must take into account the estimated costs of completing a home purchase transaction. These include:

- **Provincial Property Purchase Taxes. In both Ontario and British Columbia, these are very substantial**.

For a Buyer in BC, this cost will be 1% for the first $200,000 of value, and 2% on any remaining value over $200,000.

If we assume a $390,000 purchase in BC, this makes the tax component a very substantial $5800 ($2,000 plus $3,800), payable on your behalf, by your Lawyer or Notary, on closing. We'll include this $5800 cost in our example.

- **Property Tax and Other Adjustments**. You will be closing the deal in late June. The taxes for that calendar year are due July 1. This means you will be paying all the property taxes for the entire year. Therefore the Seller will owe you almost half of the tax bill due to his residency of almost six months.

Since what the Seller will owe you will more than offset any utility or other adjustments, we will allow **zero** cost to you on closing. **Remember however, to budget for that tax bill!**

- **Legal Costs**. Whether you choose a Lawyer or a Notary, he will provide you with an accurate estimate of the legal costs. These can easily total **$1,000,** the figure we'll use for our example.

d) Insurance Costs

There are a number of these to consider:

- **High-Ratio Mortgage Insurance**

  If you are a Buyer with *less* than a 20% down payment, your Lender *may* still qualify you for a *"high-ratio mortgage"*, but *only* if your household income supports such a loan.

  Existing Canadian legislation requires that any home Buyer with less than a 20% down payment, who wishes to borrow from a front-line Lender such as a Bank, Credit Union or Trust Company, must obtain insurance through either ***Canada Mortgage and Housing Corporation (CMHC) or Genworth Financial.*** This is to protect the Lender from any future default by the Borrower.

  You, the Borrower, will be required to bear the cost of this insurance, at the time of completion of your home purchase.

  Your Lender *will* permit you to add this amount to your mortgage, which means that you do not have to pay for this insurance in cash. You may however *prefer to pay this cost up front,* to avoid turning a one-time insurance cost into a 25-year debt item!

  The cost of high-ratio mortgage insurance varies with the mortgage amount insured, but it may run into several thousand dollars.

....

For our example, we'll assume that our Buyer feels that he requires *at least $380,000* to find a home that meets all of his family's *"needs"*.

This means that to take advantage of the maximum-allowable $300,000 mortgage opportunity, his $80,000 down payment would represent about 21% of the anticipated $380,000 purchase price. This qualifies him for a *conventional* mortgage and avoids the additional insurance cost of a *high-ratio* mortgage.

> *NOTE:* **As of April, 2007, the Canadian Federal Government enacted legislation which lowered the down payment threshold for a conventional mortgage from 25% to 20%. This is in recognition that rising housing costs are making home ownership more difficult, especially for the first-time Buyer.**

....

To return to our example:

- **Mortgage Life Insurance**

Some Lenders will expect you to carry mortgage life insurance, as further protection of their position. We'll assume you have sufficient *personal life insurance* that neither you, nor the Lender, require it in this instance.

It is usually far more economical to purchase separate *term life insurance* from an insurance broker to cover the Buyer's mortgage liability, than to purchase coverage from the mortgage Lender.

- **Title Insurance**

Some Buyers choose to purchase Title Insurance. This provides peace of mind that there is no hidden defect in the Title.

Even though it differs somewhat by province, Canada's Land Title system is one of the best in the world. This extra coverage is strictly discretionary. The low premium attests to the fact that this insurance is rarely called upon to pay a claim, or to defend a legal action. It will nevertheless, amount to several hundred dollars, depending on the value insured.

Emerging as the primary reason to consider this insurance is the provision, for the Buyer, of protection against fraudulent acts by another party, potentially affecting his ownership rights.

Your Lawyer or Notary can advise you on the specifics of this insurance, confirm the price, and arrange it for you, should you choose to purchase it. We'll assume for our example, a cost of $400, and that our Buyer elects to purchase this added protection.

- **Home Insurance**

Always carry insurance on your home from the moment you become the owner!

If you have a mortgage, your Lender will require confirmation of adequate home insurance, as one of the conditions of his loan.

Any Insurance Broker will provide you with an estimate, to assist in your budgeting. We'll assume this estimate, for our example, is $900.

e) Moving Costs

These can vary from a few hundred dollars, if your move is a local one with friends helping, to several thousand dollars if it is an out-of-town relocation requiring professional assistance. A moving company will be glad to come to your home, to give you an estimate for planning purposes. Let's assume $2,000 is the estimated moving cost in our example.

If you are less mobile, or for any other reason, in need of comprehensive moving assistance, be aware that in most larger communities, professional firms exist which will organize and handle your move from start to finish. The cost of this service is in addition to your normal moving costs, but may well be worth it in some circumstances.

f) Inspection, Appraisal, and Property Survey Costs

As a Buyer you are almost always well-advised to commission an inspection prior to firming up any offer to purchase. Let's assume we know of an excellent Inspector who will charge only $200. We'll use this in our example.

The Mortgage Lender will often require the Buyer to pay for the appraisal of your proposed purchase, and for a Survey Certificate, if the Seller does not provide one.

The house appraisal assures the Lender that the property has the necessary value in support of the mortgage amount.

The Survey Certificate shows the legal boundaries of the property, any easement or right-of-way, and the exact location of all permanent structures.

For our example, we will use $200 as the cost of appraisal. Since a Survey Certificate is usually available from the Seller, we assume that a new one is not required for our example.

…………………………..

g) Crunching The Numbers

Armed with the above information, our Buyer can now calculate, with a high degree of accuracy, what he can *really* afford to spend on the purchase of his next home.

Our calculation in this example would show:

Buyer's Available Funds:

Down Payment	$ 80,000
Mortgage	$ 300,000
Savings Bond	$ 10,000
Total Funds Available	$ 390,000

Buyer's Closing Costs:

Property Purchase Tax	$ 5,800
Property Tax & Other Adjustments	$ 0
Legal Costs	$ 1,000
High-Ratio Mortgage Insurance Costs	$ 0
Mortgage Life Insurance	$ 0
Title Insurance	$ 400
Home Insurance	$ 900
Moving Costs	$ 2,000
Inspection Costs	$ 200
Appraisal Costs	$ 200
Total Closing Costs	$ 10,500

By subtracting his expected *closing costs* from his available *funds*, this calculation indicates that our Buyer's **maximum purchase price** for his next home is **$379,500.**

> **REMEMBER......His *maximum purchase price* is probably the most important item of information the Buyer needs *before* he proceeds with a serious search for his next home.**

BUT.... before launching into that final search for the perfect home solution, one other important issue remains to be considered.

REALTOR OR NO REALTOR?

This is the same question we asked ourselves when planning to sell.

When ***purchasing*** a home in Canada, one huge difference exists when working with a Realtor, compared to when one is selling. There is usually *zero* cost to the Buyer when using a Realtor to assist with a purchase.

Most homes are sold under the *Multiple Listing Service*, in which case the listing Realtor shares *his* commission with any other Realtor who successfully introduces a Buyer. It is the *home Seller* who pays the entire commission cost.

In most cases therefore, it makes sense to enlist a professional Realtor to assist you in finding and purchasing your ideal home.

You may recently have sold your home. Were you satisfied with your Realtor's performance?

If so, why not retain him for this important next step? You may even have negotiated a "side letter," as described in Chapter Four, which reduces your selling commission if the same Realtor helps to secure your replacement home.

More important perhaps, is that retaining a professional Realtor helps to even the playing field during negotiations on the home of your choice. Do *you* personally want to negotiate with the Realtor who has the home listed for sale? While that Realtor would be required to secure a "Dual Agency Agreement" from both the Seller and you, the Buyer, and be bound to act ethically toward both parties, the fact remains that he has a huge edge in information, and probably negotiating skill, over you.

You want someone who is working for you, and *only* for you!

CHAPTER TWELVE

SELECTING A REALTOR

If you have just sold successfully, you are more likely to choose to represent you, the Realtor who assisted in your sale.

However, if you were not satisfied with the overall effectiveness of that Realtor, if you are relocating to another community, or if you are becoming a homeowner for the first time, you will have to select your Realtor carefully.

You will not be paying the bill for retaining this Realtor. He will be sharing the commission, paid by the Seller to the Listing Agent. That however, is no reason to be careless in your Realtor selection process.

You can not predict the calibre of the Listing Realtor for the home you eventually choose to purchase. He could be one of the top-selling Realtors in the entire area. You want *your* Realtor to be at least as effective!

To successfully select a Realtor, follow the guidelines outlined in Chapter Three. Confirm a potential Realtor's credentials and track record:

- Is he visibly successful?
- Does he sell regularly in the neighbourhoods in which you are interested?
- Does he provide references from other Buyers he has served?
- Have you seen the Realtor in action at his own open houses?
- How effective was he in his interactions with you and other visitors?

- Is his personality compatible with yours?
- Perhaps most importantly, does he *listen* to you, the potential Buyer?

Ensure that the Realtor who will be working for you has *a proven track record,* and can hold his own in representing you, in the eventual negotiating process.

Choose a Realtor who will not waste your time. Why trudge through numerous homes which are totally unsuitable to your family's needs, or which are unaffordable?

If you have just sold, and are under some time pressure due to a looming closing date, you need someone to guide you in a *focused search,* which enables you to make a relatively prompt, yet careful selection. Indeed, you will, hopefully, have been screening houses, even *before* your house sold. If so, you may well have a house or two in mind for a closer look.

Once you have a potential Realtor in mind, *whether you have worked with him previously or not,* invite him to your home. Share with him all of your tentative calculations and conclusions pertinent to buying a house. Discuss your "*needs*" and your "*wants*", as well as your *maximum purchase price.*

Review your logic with him. How does he respond? Does he make helpful suggestions which allow you to refine your own analysis? Does he provide useful insight about the potential of the marketplace to meet *your* requirements? And, most importantly, does he really *listen* to you, and do his comments reflect that?

If you are comfortable with the outcome of your meeting, confirm your expectations and commit to working with that Realtor, as long as he clearly operates within the outlined framework.

In some areas of Canada, where *Buyer's Agency Contracts* are the norm, the Realtor will want you to execute a formal agreement which binds you to him for a period of time. I personally would avoid signing such a contract. In most instances the Realtor will still agree to work with you regardless of the existence of a formal contract.

Remember that, unlike with a *Listing Agreement's* necessary commitment, if you are not locked into the relationship for a specific period of time when buying a house, you are in the driver's seat. If the Realtor's performance, during your home search, does not impress you, there is nothing to prevent your looking for a different Realtor. Realtors know this and generally, will work very hard to keep you impressed.

In reality, if you have been careful in your selection process, it should be the very rare instance when you need to change Realtors. *But it is good to know that you have that option!*

…………………………………..

As a Realtor, I never ceased to be amazed when other Realtors spoke in frustration of clients to whom they had shown dozens of homes, without finding one on which to make an offer.

I suspect that a good part of the reason for the numerous showings was a lack of listening skills on the part of the Realtor. This, in turn, led to the showing of homes that had no chance of meeting their clients' basic "needs", let alone their "wants".

I too, had a few clients who absolutely insisted on seeing a large number of homes, but they were the rare exception. Most of the time, a client found a suitable home after viewing six to eight houses. It may on occasion, have taken some time waiting for the right house, but I tried to not waste the Buyer's time, nor mine, by showing them every available house.

The key was that right from the outset, I worked with the client to clearly identify both his "needs" and his "wants". I then tried to carefully select only those homes which met his minimum "needs" – including his price range. As a result, every home that I showed my client, represented a true, potential solution. The final decision often came down to choosing the home that also met many of the Buyer's "wants".

CHAPTER THIRTEEN

YOUR SEARCH

Hopefully, while your home was on the market, *or* as a first-time Buyer before you began searching in earnest, you followed some of the hints of earlier chapters, becoming tuned into the housing market.

You probably kept your eye on listings, checked related websites, read the advertisements, and even visited various open houses, particularly in your target area.

....

Now that you have chosen your Realtor, giving him a clear understanding of your expectations, it's time to become more focused. Your "*needs*" and "*wants*", clearly defined, are in the forefront of both your and your Realtor's minds.

You are now ready to move into high gear, to actually search for *the* home that meets your needs.

1. YOUR APPROACH

a) **Ask your Realtor for a detailed information sheet** for each home listed in the general area *and* price range you have selected. Ensure that you receive immediate updates of *all* new listings which appear to meet your requirements. Absorb this information carefully.

b) **Drive by every listing** the Realtor gives you. Have a pencil and the listing sheet in hand. Rule out those you *know* you would not consider, based on your drive-by reaction. If you don't like the street or neighbourhood, the appearance or style, scratch it off your list!

c) **On your computer, scan the MLS listings** for the area in which you are interested. You may spot a home that is of interest, but which your Realtor did not include. Similarly, carefully examine the local real estate publication. Scrutinize the list of open houses scheduled for the coming weekend.

d) **Drive around. Attend open houses** in your specific areas of interest. Don't limit yourself to only those which appear to meet your specific requirements. Part of the exercise is to increase your knowledge of the market. This will help you better appreciate the relative value of the house you eventually select as best meeting your needs.

a) If **a home that you visit at an open house is on your list of possibilities**, spend enough time in it to make one of two decisions:

- Confirm that it is a possibility;
- Rule it out entirely.

REMEMBER...... When visiting open houses without your Realtor, always tell the attending Realtor, the name of the Realtor with whom you are working.

This will avoid future misunderstandings about your Realtor's entitlement to represent you, and to a share of the commission, should you subsequently decide to make an offer on that particular house.

Not only is it fair to your Realtor, but also, it protects *your* interests by having your own Realtor to negotiate on *your* behalf.

f) **On your own, you may find one or two "possibles."** Ask your Realtor to arrange a private showing, with himself also in attendance. He will add these to the list of showings that he will be scheduling for you.

2. NARROWING THE FOCUS

Your head is reeling with information. You have been through quite a number of open houses. Your Realtor has arranged for you to view another five or six properties that are still on your list of possibilities.

How do you keep track of what you have seen in each house you visit? Do you keep detailed notes on each? *No!*

Focus *only* on the *one best possible choice* that you have viewed so far.

Whether at an open house, or attending a showing with your Realtor, follow these simple steps:

a) **Rule out the house immediately, if it does not meet your identified *needs*.**

   Don't try to remember details. It is not necessary if it is not an option for you. Keep in mind only *general* facts, as part of your overall education about the market, and values within it.

b) **Take extra time to thoroughly view the first house that appears to meet all of your basic *needs*.**

   At this stage of your search, this *one* property is now your sole focus, as your only possible home.

c) **When you come to the next house that appears to also meet your *needs*, ask yourself only two questions**:

   - ***If I HAD to choose one of these two options, which one most meets my "needs" and "wants"?***
   - ***Which of the two would I buy?***

   You may yet be far from making a decision to buy. This exercise however, will keep you focused on your *one best solution*, at this point in your search!

   Continue this process until you have *exhausted all reasonable choices*, and are assured that you really have zeroed in on the *best option available.*

   It is possible that you will end up with two equally promising options. Each may meet not only all your "*needs*", but also satisfy a significant number of your "*wants*".

To have several possible choices is ideal. It allows you to be confident during subsequent negotiations, that if agreement can not be reached on your first choice, you do have a good back-up alternative.

Whether you have narrowed your search to one, or to several options, do not as yet, charge ahead with an offer!

d) **Ask your Realtor to arrange a second showing of your one or two most promising choices.**

Have him ask the owner if you may take photos. The owner will know that with a second showing, you are a serious prospect. He will probably have no problem with your taking photographs. Take advantage of this approval. Take dozens of pictures from all angles, of the yard, the home's exterior, and of each interior room. You will find the photos to be an invaluable tool when you return home, to help recollect details that you would never remember from memory.

Consider your camera as another set of eyes with a built-in memory!

Should you eventually end up buying that home, you will already have, in the photos, an excellent record of details with which to plan decor and furniture layouts, during the weeks leading up to your actual occupancy

e) **After your second viewing, go home. Discuss it, recheck it against your "needs" list, study your photos, and sleep on it!**

If the next day, you are still keen on the house, it will probably be a good decision to proceed with an offer.

Don't be shy however, to request a third viewing, if you have any doubt at all!

You are, after all, about to spend *hundreds of thousands of dollars* on a house in which you may live for the next ten years, or longer! Do not apologize for wanting to have another look. You may wish to have other members of your family with you, to obtain their opinion, or you may simply want to double-check your own comfort level with the house.

....

WHAT *NOT* TO DO! ***One of my more memorable experiences:***

I was the listing agent on a $550,000 home, located on First Nations land, on a 99-year prepaid lease in a residential suburb of about 100 exclusive homes. The Sellers had moved to Ottawa, leaving the house totally empty, except for a kitchen table. A hard sell at the best of times!

About one hour into my first open house, an older gentleman drove up in a Cadillac, strolled in, and spent about five minutes walking through the home. He then turned to me and said, "Yup, I'll take it! How much?", as if he were buying a loaf of bread!

Since he was not represented by an agent, I explained my "Dual Agency" responsibilities to both Buyer and Seller. I also outlined that normally, a Buyer would make an offer, with appropriate conditions, to which the Seller would then respond.

The gentleman was not interested in the caution, insisting that he not only write a cheque immediately, but that the offer would have no conditions. Furthermore, he added that he wanted to complete the deal, and occupy the home within a few days!

Having properly cautioned him on normal practices and, after obtaining his signature on the "Dual Agency Agreement" (which I also faxed to the Seller for signature), I finally helped him write his offer of $525,000, with no conditions.

The Sellers were only too happy to accept! The deal closed within a week.

....

Subsequently, I learned that the Buyer was a very successful First Nations fisherman who had moved off the Reserve the previous year. That particular week he had earned $600,000, during the annual herring fishery. His accountant had told him, on the same day as my open house, that he had better move back onto the Reservation before December 31, or he would be paying $300,000 of his profits in taxes!

Even though this was only summer, the first thing my Buyer did after leaving his accountant, was to drive up to the area where I was holding my open house, because it qualified as "Reservation Lands". He bought the first house that he came upon!

As you will recognize, this is an extreme example. While I tried to be scrupulously professional and fair to both the impatient Buyer and my Sellers, there is no doubt that this Buyer would have been much wiser to first retain his own Realtor, explain his key "need", and give himself time over the next several months, to achieve a best-value solution.

While this is a rather unusual example, I encountered many other instances when a Buyer was ready to make an offer without, in my opinion, being sufficiently prepared to do so. This became particularly noticeable during periods of a "Seller's Market", when the Buyer was afraid of losing an opportunity to purchase a particular house.

REMEMBER...... Do not be stampeded into making a quick offer! Do not get so excited about a particular home, that you leave your common sense behind!

CHAPTER FOURTEEN

YOUR OFFER

Finally! You have identified a house that meets all of your *"needs"*, and even some of your *"wants"*. You have visited it two or three times. You and your family continue to feel comfortable, even excited, with the prospect of making that house your home.

You are now ready to proceed with an offer. Your Realtor will guide you through the documentation process, including issues of:

- Price
- Deposit
- Inclusions
- Dates
- Seller's Covenants
- Conditions

We'll look at each individually:

1. THE PRICE

Rarely does a home Seller expect to receive a full-price offer. Indeed, this seldom occurs.

That does not mean however, that you, the Buyer, should be flippant about your offer. Remember your own expectations and reactions when you were selling!

Be reasonable in your approach, if you want the Seller to also respond reasonably. If you and your Realtor have agreed that your target home is exceptionally well-priced, offer accordingly, perhaps 2 to 4% below asking price.

Consider your Realtor's advice carefully. If it is an exceptionally *"hot"* Seller's market, and you really want this house, you will probably have to offer much closer to the asking price, even if not on your first-round offer.

On the other hand, if the house is clearly priced too high for the existing market, make an offer that is somewhat below what your, and your Realtor's, research indicates to be a realistic value.

The *length of time* the home has been on the market is also a consideration. A home that has been available for months may well lead a Buyer to begin with a significantly lower offer.

"Low-balling" the offer however, on a well-priced home which has just been listed, may offend unnecessarily, and possibly weaken your negotiating position.

You want a nice home, but you also want it to become a reasonable *investment.* In some circumstances, walking away may be your best option. If you have been fair with your offer and counter-offer, and the Seller refuses to be reasonable in his responses, consider walking away. Although you should rarely have to, be prepared to do so!

REMEMBER..... Unless you are loaded with excess cash, do not be so taken with a particular house that you end up paying a totally unrealistic price for it.

2. DEPOSIT

A key requirement of any contract is that there be "consideration". This simply means that the Buyer must offer *value* as part of the contract. The *deposit* meets that legal requirement. It also serves as a guarantee of performance.

If you have the financial ability to write a significant cheque, offer a substantial deposit "on acceptance". A five-to-ten percent offered deposit will impress a Seller, as an indication of your seriousness and financial strength.

REMEMBER..... The deposit becomes non-refundable only *after* all conditions are removed.

If the deal does not proceed because of an unfulfilled condition, the contract terminates, and the Realtor must immediately return your deposit.

3. INCLUSIONS

Again, be reasonable in your approach to items that the Seller is offering to include or exclude. If he really wants the chandelier or the appliances, let him take them – unless you are prepared to move toward his asking price. It is always best to *focus on the more important issues*, primarily price and conditions, rather than to get too concerned with lesser issues.

REMEMBER..... Any reasonable exclusion can be replaced with the dollars you save on the purchase price of your home!

4. DATES

If you have recently sold your home, you will obviously wish to insert in your *Offer to Purchase*, dates which complement your *selling* dates, thereby allowing you to move seamlessly, from one home to the next.

Sellers generally understand this, and will often be able to accommodate a Buyer's date requirements. It is normal, and possible, for the completion and possession dates for the two transactions to coincide.

Essentially, as the Buyer's moving van arrives in the driveway of your sold house, yours passes it as it pulls out, on the way to your new home, where you then encounter the Seller as he is moving out! Not unlike the passing of the baton in a relay race.

Although the logistics can be tricky, it always seems to work out. Your Realtor has seen this many times, and will guide you appropriately on the dates.

If you are moving into your first home from a rental property, you *may* be somewhat more flexible on dates, and able to be more accommodating to the requirements of the Seller.

It is most unusual for negotiations to fall apart, based only on disagreements over dates. A few telephone calls between the two Realtors can informally work out dates, sometimes even before they are included in your offer.

5. SELLER'S COVENANTS

It is quite acceptable for a Buyer to specify a number of *expectations* that he may have of the Seller in a particular transaction. The following are examples:

- "The vendor will, at his cost, provide the purchaser with a Survey Certificate of the property, within five days of the date of acceptance of the offer."
- "The attached Property Condition Disclosure Statement, dated April 6, 2007, is incorporated into this contract, and forms an integral part thereof."

Note that these are reasonable *expectations*, rather than *conditions* which are addressed next.

6. CONDITIONS

In Chapter Eight we addressed the importance when selling your home, of adequately understanding and dealing with conditions attached to an offer.

This is even more important when you are *buying a home.*

REMEMBER.......The fewer conditions attached to your offer to buy, the more appealing it will be to the Seller.

Imposing fewer conditions tends to improve your bargaining power, particularly on price. While you keep this fact in mind, you must also ensure that you *protect yourself* adequately in any offer, in order to be 100% certain, that should the Seller accept without any changes, you will be able to carry through on all of your offered commitments. For example:

- **Financing**

If you are able to purchase the home without the need for a mortgage, you obviously do not need a "Subject to Financing" clause. This will impress a Seller because he is assured that you are strong financially, and able to *complete*, should he accept your offer.

If you *do* require a mortgage, but for less than half the value of the home, *and* your Lender has assured you that you qualify for such an amount, you can also *consider* dispensing with a financing condition.

However, should your mortgage requirements exceed 50% of value, be prudent. *Always* include a financing condition, to ensure that no untoward surprises ensue from your Lender.

- **Inspection**

Most home Sellers will expect an offer to include a "Subject to Inspection" condition. If not, their Realtor will explain that this is normal practice, and to be expected.

Only if *you* are an *expert* in home inspections, and have spent enough time in your prospective home during the viewing process, to be satisfied with the condition of the home, should you consider not including such a condition. This applies even if purchasing a newly-built home!

I have seen the results of inspections on newly-built homes with occupancy permits, in which the inspection identified issues involving thousands of dollars!

- **Title Review**

Most listing Realtors will routinely give a potential Buyer's Realtor a "State of Title" information sheet listing any encumbrances on the property. If not, the Buyer should add a "Subject to Title Review" condition. A Buyer should always review this document as part of his due diligence on a property, thus ensuring that he is aware of any easements or rights-of-way, and that they do not impair his plans for the land.

A Buyer need not concern himself with the Seller's financial encumbrances, such as mortgages or lines of credit, which are secured by the property, because it is the job of the Buyer's Lawyer or Notary to ensure their removal from title, prior to turning over payment for the transaction.

- **Subject to Sale**

You will significantly weaken your negotiating power and indeed, your likelihood of achieving a deal, if you include a "*Subject to Sale*" condition. The reasons were addressed in Chapter Eight.

To reiterate, a Seller has *no certainty of a sale* even if he accepts such a condition. **Certainty is what a Seller wants!**

If you *must* include such a condition, expect to pay more for the house than you would without it.

Even after you, the Buyer, agree to pay this premium you *may* still lose your position as Buyer. Should another offer be made while you await the sale of your home, the Seller **will** invoke the "24-, 48- or 72-hour" clause which usually accompanies a "Subject to Sale" condition. If you then fail to firm up the purchase, you no longer have a chance on this house.

More often than not, a "Subject to Sale" condition fails to lead to the successful sale that was intended when the offer was first written and accepted.

If at all possible, *sell your house first*, then make the offer! This will result in better value for you every time.

The one exception to this rule is if you are financially so strong that you are in the enviable position of not *having* to sell first, and you absolutely *must have* that particular house. It is then, that you might choose to make an offer with only an "inspection" condition.

If you do proceed without a financing condition, be sure that *either* you have enough funds on hand to complete the deal, if it is accepted, *or* you have the necessary "interim financing" pre-arranged with your Lender.

REMEMBER..... Sellers will routinely expect and accept *"financing"* and *"inspection"* conditions.

You, the Buyer, are always prudent to include them, as long as they are accompanied by reasonable time frames for removal, perhaps five to ten working days.

On the other hand, ***Sellers do not like "Subject to Sale"*** conditions. Try to avoid them!

CHAPTER FIFTEEN

THE NEGOTIATIONS

You have submitted what you and your Realtor have determined to be a good starting offer.

You have now entered the crucial *negotiations* phase.

This is both an exciting, and somewhat tense, stage on your road to the successful purchase of your ideal home.

Fortunately, the time frames allowed for acceptance of each offer and counter-offer, are usually a matter of *hours*. This process however, may drag out over two, three, or more offers and counter-offers, each with its own time frame for acceptance.

It may well be *several days* before a final sign-off occurs and you secure the rights to the house, subject only to *your* being satisfied with *your* conditions, and occasionally, the Seller with his condition.

In most cases however, both parties wish the process to conclude quickly, often managing to do so on the same day that the offer is presented. You may experience a late night, but it is worth it to achieve a *deal in principle*, for the house that you want.

Always keep in mind that the Seller wants to sell his home, as much as you want to buy it.

Don't let yourself become frustrated with the process! Negotiations may take bizarre twists and turns. You may even feel offended at times! *Do not walk away from a negotiation*, unless you have confirmed, absolutely, that there is *no* chance of a mutually acceptable compromise.

The challenge for all parties – the Seller, the two Realtors, and you, the Buyer – is to determine whether a compromise can be struck which satisfies both Buyer and Seller. This is no easy task! With *four* parties working to arrive at a consensus position for two of them, human dynamics often interfere with what can be a smooth process. Be patient and try not to be offended. It may indeed be that *your* best offer, usually on price, simply does not satisfy the minimum acceptable position of the Seller, at least at this point in the life of his listing.

If you *must* walk away from a home you would love to own, try to do so on *good* terms.

Have your Realtor advise the Seller's Realtor that you simply are not able to improve on your last counter-offer, but that you have appreciated the Seller's efforts in the negotiations. You may be surprised! Sometimes the Seller will sleep on it and, next morning, have his Realtor contact yours to advise that he will accept your last position!

*This can happen within hours of the Buyer **politely** walking away!*

Avoid this approach as simply a negotiating tactic, thinking that you may get a better deal. In most cases, you will *not* hear back from the Seller. If you are determined to have the house, it is *you* who will then have to back down, and agree to the Seller's last position. Had you originally continued the negotiations, you may have been able to split the difference in some manner, thereby obtaining a better deal than that upon which you settled.

The complexities and the subtleties of negotiations are key reasons why you are well advised to have a good Realtor representing you.

He will be able to act on *your* behalf, objectively and unemotionally providing leadership during the process, which should ultimately result in an agreement.

REMEMBER.....Each time you make a change to the contract, you are returning control of the negotiations, back to the other party.

Your Realtor will remind you, every time one party changes *so much as a comma*, on an offer or counter-offer, that offer is dead and off the table, unless the other party initials the change that was made, or writes a new offer.

This is a major reason why your Realtor will be advising you on how aggressively to pursue certain points.

If, for example, during negotiations on a $400,000 home, you are within $1,000 of an agreement, you may be well-advised to accept, rather than try for another $500 reduction. It is no longer a significant difference. Letting the Seller feel good that his last position prevailed, may well work in your interest. If you later need some small accommodation from him, such as adjusting the occupancy date by a day because of an unexpected problem with your move, he may be more amenable to agreeing.

REMEMBER..... The ideal contract is one in which both parties are smiling, and each feels satisfied that he did well!

Refer back to Chapter Eight for a refresher on the negotiation process.

CHAPTER SIXTEEN

SATISFYING THE CONDITIONS

Both Buyer and Seller must keep in mind that:

A contract which has been accepted and signed by both parties is *NOT* final and binding upon either of them, until *ALL* conditions which were in the contract are satisfied, *AND* removed within the time frame set out in the contract.

As a Buyer, you must be as diligent in removing your conditions on a timely basis, as you were in negotiating the contract itself. Your considerations will include:

- Buyer's Conditions
- Seller's Conditions
- Buyer's "Inspection" Condition
- Selecting a Home Inspector
- Inspection Process
- Buyer's "Financing" Condition

1. BUYER'S CONDITIONS

If the conditions on an accepted contract are solely yours, the Buyer's, *and if they were properly written*, you are in full control of the outcome.

While *you* still have an "escape hatch" from the deal, through any one of your conditions, the Seller does not. He is 100% legally bound by the contract. His ability to back out is limited only to any failure on your part as Buyer, to remove all of *your* conditions within the time frame specified.

Notice the phrase "*if they were properly written*". For *you* to have sole control of each of *your* conditions, the following statement must be included with each:

"This condition is for the sole benefit of the Buyer".

With the inclusion of these words, it is at the sole discretion of the Buyer, whether or not he performs as originally intended in the condition.

An example: The Buyer chooses to *not* carry through on an inspection, which was one of his conditions.

As long as the Buyer removes that condition by the time and date specified, the Seller can not back out of the contract by arguing that the Buyer failed to do an inspection. Furthermore, the Buyer's signature on the removal of the condition, is all that is required to satisfy it. A further signature from the Seller is often obtained, but is not legally required.

If this crucial "sole benefit" statement is not included, the Seller is presented with a potential avenue of escape from his commitment, by his simple refusal to sign off on the Buyer's subject removal. In the absence of such a clause, the Seller's signature *would* be required.

2. SELLER'S CONDITIONS

As referred to above, instances may occur when the contract you have accepted contains a condition written by the Seller *"for his sole benefit"*. A typical example might be:

"Subject to the Seller reaching an agreement fully satisfactory to him on the purchase of 1055 Parklane Street, on or before Friday, March 16, 2006. This condition is for the sole benefit of the Seller."

In this case, the Seller in all likelihood, had narrowed the search for his replacement home to 1055 Parklane Street. Before making an offer on that house, he was waiting only on the firm sale of his current house at 22 Cedar Street. Now he requires a short period of time, usually not exceeding a few days, to finalize the purchase of the Parklane property.

In such an instance, your Seller of Cedar Street, in negotiating an offer on his target house at 1055 Parklane, will want to include his own condition along the following lines:

"Subject to the Buyer (of 1055 Parklane) having all conditions associated with the sale of his home at 22 Cedar Street

removed on or before (the last date for removal of subjects that you had specified on the purchase of his home). This condition is for the sole benefit of the Buyer."

By including this condition in *his* purchase, your Seller is protecting himself from the possibility that your condition or conditions will not be removed, thus causing his sale to collapse. He does not expect it to happen, but it could!

If both the Buyer and the Seller have conditions to be satisfied before the contract becomes firm and binding, then neither is solely in control of the outcome. Each party must take specific action to remove *his* conditions, before being legally bound by the contract.

It is not necessary for *you* to understand in depth all of these legal realities. It is your Realtor who is obliged to explain them, and to properly manage them for you.

This is a further illustration of the importance of choosing the right Realtor, and of the potential pitfalls of attempting to sell or buy without the professional assistance of a competent one.

3. BUYER'S INSPECTION CONDITION

This is a crucial condition for you as a Buyer. It *must* be treated seriously, and with great care.

Take full advantage of your opportunity to retain a professional Inspector to thoroughly examine your proposed home. He will fully brief you on its condition, so that you are not unwittingly buying into a major repair or maintenance issue.

The objectives of this inspection are several:

- **To *verify* the representations made by the Seller in his Property Condition Disclosure** document, received from him through your Realtor.

You are not trying to catch the Seller in an untruth. Rather, you are recognizing that he was providing his best judgement on his home's condition. Never having experienced a problem with his roof, he may have honestly felt that the roof was good for another ten years.

Since the house is only twelve years old, this may have been an entirely reasonable conclusion on his part.

A professional Inspector however, upon examining the roof very closely, *may* conclude that the roof needs to be replaced much sooner than anticipated.

Although this information may not stop you from buying the house, it does prevent your being blindsided by an unsuspected, emerging expense.

- **To carefully check that there are no "latent defects"** which neither you nor the Seller would normally notice. *A latent defect is an inherent flaw or weakness in the house which is not easily detected by routine examination.*

  Examples might include:

  a) The presence of aluminium wiring, which no longer meets code requirements in new construction. It can be made safe by relatively minor modifications by an electrician, usually at a cost of between $1,000 and $2,000.

  b) The presence of asbestos or urea formaldehyde in older homes. These are rarely seen today, but if present, certainly fall into the "deal breaker" category.

  c) Evidence of current or past carpenter ant, or other pest, activity.

  d) Evidence of current or past moisture problems.

- **To provide you with a comprehensive written report**, detailing the present condition of the house, identifying not only major issues, but also minor maintenance items which should be addressed.

....

As a rule, your home Inspector will not be qualified to inspect, or advise on, the condition of specialized items such as a swimming pool, hot tub, elevator, or septic system. Should any of these be present in your target home, retain the appropriate specialist to have them inspected. Yes, this will add to the cost of your inspection.

The prudent Buyer should not proceed with a purchase, without being fully informed on *every* aspect of the home. *Who needs unpleasant, costly surprises as he settles into his new home?*

4. SELECTING A HOME INSPECTOR

Given the significance of an inspection, it is important to select a professional Inspector with extensive *residential* experience; one who belongs to, and is in good standing with, **The Canadian Association of Home and Property Inspectors (CAHPI).**

Be aware that in many provinces, home Inspectors are not yet regulated; in those provinces, ***anyone*** *can call himself a home Inspector!*

Your Realtor may recommend a perfectly reliable Inspector, but do check around. Ask your friends whom they used, and how satisfied they were. Check references if possible, but remember, do so quickly, in order to meet the time line for removal of the inspection condition.

The well-prepared Buyer will have done his homework on Inspectors prior to or during his home search. He may, in fact, have contacted a specific Inspector to stand by for a call. Once he actually requires the Inspector, the Buyer can then schedule the inspection within a few days.

5. THE INSPECTION PROCESS

During the inspection, your Realtor will have arranged for the Seller to vacate his home. This is normal etiquette to ensure an undisturbed and objective inspection. Either your Realtor, or the owner's Realtor, will let the Inspector into the house.

You, the Buyer, should also refrain from visiting until perhaps, the last hour of the inspection. Your Inspector needs to focus his effort, and not be disturbed by your presence and questions.

Rest assured, he will give you a comprehensive briefing and tour at the end of his inspection.

Should you arrive before the Inspector is ready for you, greet him but then stay out of his way. Explore the yard, the house exterior, or areas of the home where he is not working.

Your Inspector will take two to four hours to *thoroughly* inspect your prospective home.

....

The Inspector has documented his findings, and is now ready to brief you in some detail.

REMEMBER..... You are paying the Inspector to find deficiencies, so expect to hear that some do exist! No house will be perfect.

Invite your Realtor to be present for the briefing session. The detailed report will tune him in thoroughly, should follow-up action with the Seller become necessary.

After reviewing all his findings and answering your questions, the Inspector will probably tell you **how this home compares to other homes of a similar age.** Listen very carefully. If he does not volunteer this information, ask for it!

If, even with some deficiencies, the house ranks *average or better*, for homes of that age, you probably have little cause for concern and can think seriously about removing your inspection condition.

On the other hand, if it ranks at the low end of the scale, with **deficiencies** that are substantial, costly *and* unexpected, you have a number of options before you:

- Walk away from the house, even though it was your first choice and you still like it very much. *Not a good idea without first exploring other options, unless the deficiencies are very major and bordering on scary.*
- Accept the deficiencies, plan to pay the price of correcting them, and remove the inspection condition. *Again, not a recommended option, since there may be a much better solution.*
- Have your Realtor thoroughly brief the Seller's Realtor, to verbally explore the Seller's willingness to share the cost of repairs. *This may be your best option.*

Usually such cost-sharing would come in the form of an agreed price adjustment to the originally negotiated price. This is an extremely sensitive matter for both parties. The skills of the two Realtors, in diplomacy and communication, will be severely tested if a successful outcome is to be the result.

Until a final solution is agreed upon, it may be best that these negotiations be handled verbally.

The purpose of an inspection is not to provide an excuse to renegotiate the agreed price, except in a few truly significant instances when a failure to adjust the price would cause a prudent Buyer to walk away from the deal.

> **REMEMBER..... No house will be free of flaws! It is quite normal to identify *some* defects in every home.**

Even *newly-built homes* will have a deficiency list. In those cases, a reputable Builder will usually agree to remedy everything identified, since he is selling you a brand new home that you logically would expect to be defect-free.

This is not the case with a *resale* home. Reasonable wear and tear over time is to be expected, whether buying a used car or a resale home.

6. THE BUYER'S "FINANCING" CONDITION

A *well-prepared* Buyer will have a thorough understanding of his financial capability.

He will know the amount of his mortgage eligibility, based on his expected down payment, his debts and his income. When he makes an offer, he will do so, reasonably sure that his Lender will in fact, come through with the necessary loan to complete the purchase.

Nevertheless, the *financing condition* is a good precaution, particularly if the borrowed amount exceeds 50% of the home's value.

....

Once you have made a deal on a specific home, forward a copy of the contract to your Lender. He will want to send his own Appraiser, *at your cost*, to independently confirm that the valuation is consistent with the price you are paying.

It may relieve you to know that, of hundreds of transactions, I do not recall a single instance of this process emerging as a problem.

The Lender's Appraiser generally requires less than 30 minutes of access to the home. He will not expect the Seller to leave the house during the appraisal.

The Appraiser will communicate his findings to the Lender, verbally usually within 24 hours, and in writing within a few days.

Only *after* the Lender advises you that the loan you require is *approved*, should you remove your financing condition.

....

REMEMBER..... The time frames on conditions will often run concurrently.

It is not unusual to proceed with inspection of the property at the same time that a property Surveyor or Lender's Appraiser is doing his work.

CHAPTER SEVENTEEN

THE DEAL IS MADE!

All conditions have been removed within the prescribed time frames. Both the Seller and the Buyer now have a firm and binding agreement. Neither party can amend, nor walk away from the deal, without the signature of the other party.

....

Occasionally, a Buyer fails to fully appreciate the extent of his *legal* obligation.

To illustrate, once again with a true anecdote:

A wealthy, elderly couple had lived in their home since it was new, some 30 years earlier. They knew the time was coming, when they would no longer be able to manage their current property.

They did not wish however, to list their home for sale before finding a suitable replacement townhouse, in a specific, gated community. They retained me as their Realtor.

After several weeks, a new listing, which seemed to meet all of their needs, appeared on the market. It was exceptionally well-priced. I knew it would sell very quickly.

Within hours we had viewed the home. My clients fell in love with it on the spot, and wanted to make an immediate offer.

The townhouse was only three years old. The Seller had provided a copy of a very clean, professional Inspection Report, which he had commissioned at his own expense just two months earlier, to facilitate his planned sale. As a result, my clients did not wish to have an inspection condition included in the offer.

After cautioning the couple suitably, and ascertaining that they could indeed afford to write a cheque for the full purchase price, I followed their instruction, and drafted an unconditional offer to purchase the home, with a 90-day completion and occupancy time frame.

My clients signed the offer. It was presented to the Seller, and after only one adjustment on price, the contract was signed.

Both parties were delighted to have a firm and binding agreement before day's end.

At about 3:00 a.m. that same night, my home phone rang. It was my client husband, who was extremely upset. His wife had been crying for hours, with a severe case of Buyer's remorse!

Only after they retired for the night, had she begun to grasp what their purchase meant. They would have to give up their home of 30 years, in which their entire family had grown up, and to which she was deeply attached.

Their message to me was that they no longer wanted to proceed with the deal.

You can imagine the challenge of explaining to this distraught gentleman, at 3:00 in the morning, that reversing a home purchase is not quite the same as returning a novel to a book store for a refund! Instead, I offered to visit them at 9:00 the next morning, to outline and discuss their options.

Luckily, the day dawned beautiful and sunny. Much of my clients' night-time tension had clearly eased. I explained that I could try to obtain a release for them from their commitment to purchase. I pointed out however, that it might cost them as much as the full $20,000 deposit they had tendered with their offer. They agreed to think it over, and to call me back later that day.

The end result was that they decided to honour their purchase. I immediately listed their home, which sold in three weeks, for much more than they had thought possible.

Best of all, they were absolutely delighted with their new home, once they had settled in.

....

On another occasion, one of my Buyers suffered a major financial setback, and could not complete on his contract.

His problem arose several months after he had removed all conditions on the purchase, but only weeks before the scheduled completion. He simply could not come up with the funds.

The Buyer realized as a consequence, that he could be sued for damages by the Seller, and that he had no choice but to accept that harsh reality.

Fortunately, the Seller, a Builder, was also my client in this case. Since this was a brand new home he had built, he was willing to accept the $15,000 deposit that was being held in my trust account, as full settlement of the Buyer's obligations.

This was a fair resolution, given the circumstances, leaving both parties reasonably satisfied. Less than a month later, the home sold again.

All ended well in this instance. However the Buyer was extremely fortunate in that he had not made this commitment on a ***resale*** home. In that case, the Seller might already have committed to buy a replacement home, on the strength of his sale. Had that occurred, the Buyer could have been faced with huge damages, incurred as a result of his failure to complete his purchase.

....

There are ***lessons for everyone*** in these examples:

- In the first, I, as a Realtor, should have been *more* insistent on the Buyers taking an extra day or two before proceeding, to contemplate **the real consequences** of making a firm offer.
- Both Buyer and Seller *must* be thoroughly educated by their respective Realtors, on the true meaning of a **"firm and binding agreement"**, as well as the legal and financial ramifications of breaking such an agreement.
- **Buyer's or Seller's remorse is not at all unusual.** It arises, to varying degrees, in a significant proportion of sales or purchases. In most cases, it is mild and passes quickly. Realize that *it is normal to have second thoughts!* If you have proceeded with your transaction methodically, with proper planning, and with a good Realtor, this should not emerge as a major problem.

- The second example illustrates that even when all parties proceed professionally and with due diligence through the sale and purchase process, the **unexpected *can* occur**, to challenge all parties.
- The second example also illustrates that should a legitimate issue arise, then with immediate notice of the problem, and good will on all sides, **even the toughest issues can often be resolved**, to the reasonable satisfaction of all parties.

....

WITH A FINAL UNCONDITIONAL CONTRACT IN HAND, YOU CAN NOW BEGIN TO CELEBRATE YOUR NEW HOME!

SORT THROUGH ALL THOSE PHOTOS YOU TOOK DURING THE VIEWING PROCESS, AND START PLANNING YOUR MOVE.....

CHAPTER EIGHTEEN

THE FINAL DETAILS

Time to celebrate! *However*, a few details remain. You now need to:

1. Deliver the final copy of the signed agreement to your Notary or Lawyer. He will attend to all the *transaction details*, including delivery of title to you, after the completion date.
2. Deliver a copy of the final contract to your Lender.
3. Select a moving company, or line up your friends and a truck, for the day of the move.
4. Start sorting; recycle or otherwise dispose of items that will no longer be needed.
5. Inform all service providers of the appropriate cut-off date for utilities and services associated with your sold home, as well as start-up dates at your new address.
6. Start packing!

....

About a week prior to the agreed closing date, your Notary or Lawyer will arrange an appointment with you, for the **signing of legal documents.** Once these are signed by both Buyer and Seller, they replace the original "Interim Agreement".

The Lawyer or Notary will also review with you the **Statement of Adjustments**. This will reconcile, to the penny, exactly where all funds are coming from to pay for your new home.

If, as well, you have just sold your previous residence, he will also review with you, the Statement of Adjustments for that transaction.

If, after paying for your new home, there is a surplus of funds, the Statement of Adjustments will indicate the amount of the cheque that you will receive, after the closing.

Should the Statement of Adjustments show a deficiency, meaning that further funds are required to meet the purchase price, it will specify the exact amount you must deliver, by certified cheque, at least a day or two prior to closing.

Your Lawyer or Notary may also ask if you wish to purchase **"Title Insurance".** Although we referred to this earlier, it bears repeating. For a few hundred dollars, this insurance protects you against all future title-related claims arising against your new property. In Canada, one would purchase this only for extraordinary peace of mind. Canada's Land Title system is so reliable that it is rare indeed, to hear of such an issue arising. Nothing however, is impossible, and given the low cost of this insurance, you may be happy to purchase this added peace of mind.

....

THE END RESULT......

AFTER ALL YOUR HARD WORK:

- *COMPLETION DAY FINALLY ARRIVES!*
- *YOUR NEW HOME IS NOW PAID FOR, AND LEGALLY YOURS.*
- *OCCUPANCY DATE FOLLOWS, AND YOUR MOVE IS ON.*

GIVEN THE TIME, THE EFFORT, AND THE CARE YOU EXPENDED IN THE PURCHASE PROCESS, THIS SHOULD PROVE TO BE NOT ONLY A GREAT HOME FOR YOUR FAMILY, BUT ALSO AN EXCELLENT INVESTMENT!

ENJOY YOUR NEW HOME!

THE BUYER'S 10-MINUTE SUMMARY

1. Determine the state of the market before buying. Buyer's, Seller's or Balanced Market? Adjust buying strategies accordingly.
2. Select a good Realtor. This is good business. He can add significant value to your buying process. His cost is covered by a percentage of the listing Realtor's commission.
3. Never compromise on a basic "need" when choosing a home to purchase.
4. Know your maximum comfortable purchase price *before* you begin a serious search.
5. Take great care in researching and choosing from your mortgage options. The mortgage type, interest rate, term, and amortization period will *each* have a huge, long-term impact on the total cost you end up paying for your new home.
6. Select the shortest affordable amortization period for your mortgage.
7. Carefully consider whether it is feasible to make the interest on your mortgage tax-deductible. (The "Smith Manoeuvre")
8. Use open houses as a key information-gathering tool.
9. Always tell the Realtor at an open house the name of *your* Realtor.
10. Do not be stampeded into a quick offer. Keep your emotions in check and use your common sense.
11. Do not be so taken with a particular home that you end up paying a totally unrealistic price for it.

12. Be prepared to walk away if the Seller's position is far removed from current market reality. You want a nice home but you also want it to be a solid investment.

13. Be prepared to offer a reasonable deposit "on acceptance" of your offer.

14. Any deposit you offer becomes non-refundable only *after* all conditions are removed.

15. Attach as few conditions as possible to your offer. The stronger the offer appears to the Seller, the greater your negotiating power.

16. Try to avoid a "subject to sale" offer. Sell your existing home first, then make the offer.

17. Use "financing" and "inspection" conditions to protect yourself. Sellers routinely expect these conditions.

18. Be aware that each time you make changes to a counter-offer, you are returning control to the Seller.

19. Select a professional Inspector to assess the condition of your prospective home.

20. Don't expect an inspection to produce a flawless report. In a resale house it is reasonable to find flaws pertaining to normal wear and tear.

21. Major, unexpected flaws in a house can sometimes be addressed by a reasonable adjustment to the previously-agreed price.

22. Commission an inspection of even a newly-constructed house. The Builder should be willing to remedy *every* identified defect.

23. Include a "legal review" condition "for your sole benefit" if signing a Developer's Contract of Purchase and Sale.

24. Include a *Builders Lien holdback* in any offer on a newly-constructed house. Consult with your Realtor, Lawyer or Notary on wording appropriate to the province in which you are purchasing.

25. Contemplating condominium ownership? Educate yourself on all the by-laws and regulations which you must accept in any form of "strata" ownership.

26. Carefully review the minutes of meetings and the financial statements of the "Strata Corporation", *before* firming up your offer.

27. Ensure that professional inspection of a strata unit includes not only the *unit* itself, but also the common area structures and lands for which any owner becomes proportionately responsible.

28. Take great care with an *unconditional* offer. It can achieve superb value for a Buyer, but its use must be exercised with a full appreciation of the risks that a Buyer may be assuming with such an offer.

PART IV

ADDITIONAL INSIGHTS

- **Agency Relationships**
- **More on Mortgages**
- **Buying Mortgage-Free**
- **The First-Time Home Buyer**
- **Buying or Selling a Strata Home**
- **Buying a Newly-Constructed Home**
- **Your Home As An Investment**
- ***POSTSCRIPT***

AGENCY RELATIONSHIPS

Each province has slightly different regulations which govern agency relationships in real estate transactions. The following will provide an accurate summary which is *generally* applicable to all jurisdictions.

1. Seller's Agent

A *Seller's Agent*, as the name implies, must provide exclusive loyalty to the Seller. He has a duty to the Seller to provide all possible information and advice, with the objective of obtaining the highest selling price and best possible conditions of sale.

Most Realtors whom you encounter at open houses will be Seller's Agents. If you *do* happen to fall in love with the house you are visiting, be discreet in what you say to that Agent. He has an obligation to pass on to the Seller, any insights you gave him. This includes any of your expressed thoughts on price, and what you *may* be willing to pay.

Your best strategy, other than to advise the Agent of the name of *your* Realtor, is to say very little! Instead, contact your own Realtor, have him arrange another showing with himself in attendance as well, and then proceed to plan your strategy for any ensuing offer via *your own* Realtor.

2. Buyer's Agent

Even though the *Buyer's Agent* earns his commission from the proceeds of the Seller's house sale, he is obliged to work exclusively in the best interests of the Buyer. He must keep his client's personal and financial information confidential. If the Seller's Agent lets slip some pertinent information about his Sellers, your Agent has an obligation to share it with you, if by doing so, the information can help you achieve the best possible purchase price and conditions.

3. Limited Dual Agency

In earlier chapters we referred several times to the *Dual Agency* situation. This can arise in several circumstances:

- *A Realtor has attracted both a Buyer and a Seller; both are willing to work with him in negotiating a Contract of Purchase and Sale between them.*

A typical example would be the potential Buyer who walks into an open house; he has not *beforehand* retained his own Realtor.

- *Two Realtors are involved: one has been retained by you, the Buyer; the other has been retained by the Seller.*

However, ***both*** *Realtors work for the* ***same*** *Realty or Brokerage Company, even if they do so from separate satellite offices. In this instance* ***one specific firm*** *is seen as brokering the deal between the two parties; hence the potential for a conflict of interest.*

In either of these cases, the Realtor or Realtors, must disclose to both the Buyer and Seller that *one* Agent or Company will be brokering both sides of the transaction.

If both the Buyer and the Seller are comfortable with this arrangement, after it is explained to them in detail, they must *each* indicate their acknowledgement by signing a **Limited Dual Agency Agreement**. Only after both have signed, can they be represented by the same Realtor or Brokerage Company.

The role of the Realtor in a Dual Agency situation was explained in Chapter Eight.

Every Contract of Purchase and Sale will spell out precisely, either *which* Realtor is working for *which* party, or whether it is a *Limited Dual Agency* agreement.

REMEMBER.....	**Whether you are a Buyer or a Seller, before entering into a formal agency relationship with a Realtor, be sure you understand what it means in *your* particular situation, and that your choice is *in your best interest*.**

Many books and articles can be found on the subject of mortgages. This section will not attempt to be exhaustive on all the possible options available.

However, a few key points need to be highlighted and drawn to the attention of every potential Buyer, if he is to realize *true best value* in the purchase of a home.

First, a few definitions:

Conventional Mortgage: *Is a mortgage that does not exceed 80% of the purchase price of a property.* This threshold was raised from 75% in April 2007 to assist potential home buyers trying to enter the home-ownership market.

High-Ratio Mortgage: *Is a mortgage which exceeds 80% of the purchase price.*

Mortgages which exceed this limit must be insured against default by the borrower. Canada Mortgage & Housing Corporation (CMHC) is the usual insurer, although Genworth Financial is also authorized to issue such coverage. The premium is usually between 0.65% and 2.75% of the insured value, depending on the proportion of appraised value that is insured.

Amortization Period: *Is the number of years that it would take for all regular payments to pay off the mortgage.* This is often 25 years for a new mortgage, but can be as high as 40 years.

Mortgage Term: *Is the number of years over which the agreed interest rate is applied.* Terms are usually from six months to 10 years, with 3- and 5-year terms being the most popular.

Other than the potential value swing that is available through the purchase price negotiation process, **the effective selection and negotiation of a mortgage has the greatest potential for increas-**

ing or reducing a Buyer's overall cost.

This can best be illustrated with an example:

Let's revisit our potential Buyer who requires a $300,000 mortgage.

- His Bank offers him a 5-year term, fixed-rate mortgage, with a 25-year amortization, at a 6% interest rate.
- Another Bank, or perhaps an independent mortgage Broker, can offer exactly the same mortgage, but at a 5% interest rate.

That 1% difference in interest represents almost **$2,100** annually in added cost. That amounts to a hefty **$10,500** over the first 5-year term of the mortgage! Over a 25-year amortization, the premium interest paid by the borrower would total a staggering **$52,500**!

This is certainly a difference worth shopping around for.

The posted mortgage rate at Banks is often 1% or more, above that which is available elsewhere in the market place.

Too many Buyers pay the Bank's posted rate with no attempt at negotiation. At the same time they are so cost-conscious that during the home purchase negotiations, they will risk losing the house of their choice, by haggling with a Seller over a few thousand dollars – a much lesser cost impact than paying that extra 1% for their mortgage!

A Buyer can often achieve that reduction at his own Bank, once he makes it clear that he *will* shop around for the best deal.

....

1. VARIATIONS AVAILABLE IN MORTGAGES

One could write a book on this topic alone. The market place may offer 1-, 3-, 5-, 7-, and even 10-year term mortgages, each at a different interest rate. Generally, the longer the term, the higher the rate.

Amortization options range from the most typical 25 years to 40 years. Let's examine the impact of this alluring option to lower monthly payments by opting for a 40-year amortization over the more traditional 25 years.

We'll use our same **$300,000** mortgage amount, and assume that we managed to negotiate the **5%** rate on an initial 5-year, fixed-rate mortgage. For comparison purposes we will also assume that we will get the same 5% interest rate each 5 years, when the mortgage comes up for renewal. The only difference between the two mortgages is the **25-year** versus **40-year** amortization period.

	25-Year Amortization	40-Year Amortization
Monthly Payments	**$ 1,745**	**$ 1,436**
Total Payments Over Life of Mortgage	**$ 523,500**	**$ 689,280**

The shocking results illustrate that, for the privilege of reducing a mortgage holder's *monthly* payments by **$309**, an extra **$165,780** is added to the total cost before the mortgage is fully paid off!

It's bad enough that with a 25-year amortization, the total repayments amount to **175%** of the original loan. With a 40-year amortization, this skyrockets to **230%!**

The clear lesson in this for every mortgage holder is:

- **Select the shortest affordable amortization period.**
- **If financial circumstances force you into a long amortization situation, do your utmost to increase your payments as your financial position improves, thereby shortening the period of amortization.**

These dramatic numbers also illustrate the folly of taking out a bigger mortgage than you absolutely *require* for the house you own.

To add thousands of dollars to your mortgage, in order to buy a new car or take the vacation you have always dreamed of, is a very poor economic decision. By the time you have paid off that extra borrowing as part of your mortgage, that car or vacation may have cost you several times your initial expenditure!

2. CATEGORIES OF MORTGAGES

Numerous variations in mortgage products are offered in the market place. They all tend to fit into three broad categories:

a) The Fixed-Rate Mortgage

This product *fixes* your interest rate, and hence your monthly payments, over the period of your selected term, before the mortgage comes up for renewal. Typical terms are for one, three, five, seven and ten years, with most borrowers opting for three- to five-year terms.

There are no surprises with this type of mortgage. However, if you win a lottery or inherit money, and wish to pay off the loan early, you will be subject to a substantial penalty payment.

Many Lenders of these mortgages will allow you to make one extra, annual lump sum payment of up to 10 or 15% of the outstanding principal. Generally, they will also allow you to increase your monthly payments, or to change them to a weekly or bi-weekly frequency. All of these are very helpful options to reduce the amortization period of your loan, because every extra payment you make goes directly to reduce your *principal* still owing.

b) The Variable-Rate Mortgage

With this mortgage your interest rate will *fluctuate* throughout your chosen term, as the *prime rate* moves up or down.

Generally it will be set up so that your monthly payments stay constant. More or less of your payment will go toward interest, depending on the direction of movement of the prime rate. If the rate goes up, the effect will be to lengthen your period of amortization. If the rate goes down, your amortization period will be shortened.

This is a mortgage option that should be carefully considered by every borrower.

A few years ago, Professor Moshe Milevsky of York University undertook a study of five-year rolling interest rates in Canada, during the previous 50 years.

*His study showed that **88.6%** of the time homeowners would have saved money if they held variable-rate mortgages, rather than fixed-rate mortgages. He calculated the average savings to be **$22,000** on a **$100,000** mortgage with a 15-year amortization.*

In our **$300,000** mortgage example, this would have produced an average savings of **$66,000** over a 15-year amortization period.

Despite this compelling statistic, a 2006 Royal Bank of Canada survey indicated that only 13% of those surveyed would choose a variable-rate mortgage.

Most people tend to equate a fixed-rate mortgage with peace of mind. I suspect it may be because they do not do sufficient research before selecting a mortgage.

Historically, the best value vehicle in mortgages, has been the **variable-rate mortgage**. If a Buyer has some tolerance for periodic swings in his interest rate, he would be well-advised to research this option.

The variable-rate mortgage is typically offered at a 1%, or even greater, discount from *prime rate*. Psychologically, many Buyers find this uncertainty unacceptable. They would rather lock in at a specific rate, for a specific term.

One option which Lenders are happy to offer when a customer does want the variable-rate mortgage, is to *lock* in the monthly payment, based on the then-current rate for a 3-year term mortgage. Since the rate for a 3-year term is always higher, your monthly payment will be higher than needed for the variable-rate mortgage.

This builds in a buffer to significantly reduce the impact of prime rate swings during your mortgage term. An added benefit of this approach is that the larger-than-necessary payment will *all* go toward reducing the *principal* of your mortgage. *This option is clearly worth every Buyer's serious consideration.*

c) The Open Mortgage

This product offers the holder the *full flexibility* to make *extra* payments, or even to pay off the entire mortgage at any time and without penalty. The interest rate will usually be significantly higher than other alternatives. This may be a good mortgage for you if you are expecting to come into a large sum of money in the near future.

....

Each individual must assess both his own personal comfort level and his risk tolerance, to make the best decision for *himself.* The key is to ensure that he informs himself *of all the options* and their individual consequences, before making a reasoned choice suitable for himself and his psyche.

Effort and due diligence must be applied to this process, ***BEFORE*** a home Purchase Agreement is struck, and not afterwards, when the Buyer is pressed for time and unable to shop around effectively for *his* best-value financing options.

REMEMBER....... Other than the *negotiation of purchase price of your home,* selecting wisely and *negotiating the best deal on a mortgage,* has the most significant cost impact on a Buyer.

While this may seem a strange topic to include for the many homeowners still struggling with mortgages, you too will one day, be mortgage-free, and may eventually benefit from the contents of this section.

....

A significant percentage of home purchases occurs wherein the Buyer requires no mortgage.

These fortunate Buyers, usually past age fifty, have either paid off their mortgage, or are downsizing to the degree that their existing mortgage is liquidated, as a result of the purchase of a less-expensive replacement home.

Regardless of the circumstances that place Buyers in the enviable position of buying a home for cash, they each have an extraordinary opportunity to achieve even better value, than do those who must make an offer "subject to financing".

The key reason that a "cash" Buyer sits in a stronger bargaining position, is a psychological fact. The more certain a Seller is of a firm sale, the more likely he is to compromise toward a Buyer's position, particularly on price.

....

The ultimate example of this is experienced in those rare instances when a Buyer makes a totally **unconditional offer!**

I have seen examples of such offers, wherein a very beneficial outcome resulted for the Buyer. Remember my clients who happily included all their furniture and paintings in their sale, after receiving an unconditional offer?

A Buyer *must* be cautious however, in such cases. *He waives his right to an independent inspection* in order to make an unconditional offer. A professional home Inspector, purchasing a home for himself, should be able to do this with minimal risk. Can you say the same for yourself?

The average Buyer must understand the trade-off: a stronger offer, versus the risk of unexpected expenses arising after completion. The Buyer *can reduce this risk* by bringing a home Inspector with him for the second or third viewing of his target home. Based on that cursory inspection, he can then make a judgement decision to proceed with, or without, an inspection condition.

In most circumstances, **a totally unconditional offer** should be considered only when *all* of the following exist:

- The Buyer is financially strong enough to require a minimal, or no mortgage.
- The Buyer is certain that his target home is definitely his best option.
- The Buyer is planning to tear down, or substantially renovate, the target home, thereby making an inspection unnecessary.

....

Next best to an unconditional offer, is one which contains only an *inspection* condition.

In this instance, the Seller knows that the Buyer is financially strong. If the Seller has confidence in the condition of his home, an inspection will not concern him. He will also be aware that even should the Inspector identify a major, unexpected defect, he, the Seller, can agree to a price adjustment in order to not lose the Buyer.

Such an offer however, is *not* as powerful as an unconditional offer. That is because the Buyer has an *escape hatch*, which allows him to walk away from the deal *even if the Inspection shows no major defects.* Most inspection clauses require that the Buyer be satisfied with the results to his "*sole satisfaction*". He does not have to give the Seller a specific reason for walking away.

While very few Buyers will frivolously walk away from a deal, after spending the effort and hundreds of dollars on an inspection, the fact is, they *may* do so.

The primary reason a Buyer may walk away, could be that since the day he made his original offer, he has found another home which he would really prefer to purchase.

Nevertheless, if the above three preconditions do *not* exist, a Buyer would be well-advised to include *both* an inspection and a financing condition.

Be aware that even if a Buyer's fully unconditional offer is acceptable to a Seller on price, other issues can arise with respect to dates, inclusions or other lesser matters.

It is probable that the parties, through their Realtors, would attempt to deal with such lesser issues verbally. Only after *verbal agreement* is reached on these issues, would the parties each initial a change to the deal to reflect their agreement.

If no agreement can be reached verbally, then the Seller will have to decide whether the issues are significant enough, to risk losing a firm deal. Often, he will decide that since the price is acceptable, he can live with the offer as written, and forget about further changes.

By signing acceptance of the original offer, he will have cemented a firm and binding agreement.

REMEMBER....... An *unconditional offer* which stretches the limit of acceptability on price can be a powerful means of achieving superb value for a Buyer. It must however, be used with exceptional care, and only with a full understanding of the *risks* that the Buyer is assuming.

Throughout the book we have alluded to unique issues and opportunities encountered by the first-time Buyer. This section aims to elaborate for those of you in this growing sector of the market.

1. MINIMUM DOWN PAYMENT

Many first-time Buyers will need to take advantage of the **high-ratio mortgage** option, with the required default insurance available through Canada Mortgage and Housing Corporation (CMHC), or through Genworth Financial. While this may allow them to purchase their first home with as little as zero down, striving to achieve at least a 5% down payment is prudent, if at all possible, in order to reduce extraordinary lending and insurance costs.

2. BORROWING FROM YOUR RRSP

Canadian legislation allows first-time Buyers to borrow up to $20,000 *each*, toward the down payment on their first home.

Note that since 1999, the definition of the first-time Buyer is any person or spouse or common-law partner who has not owned a home in the period beginning January 1 of the fourth calendar year preceding the year of withdrawal from an RRSP.

This definition effectively allows people to be considered as first-time Buyers more than once, as long as they have *zero* outstanding debt to their RRSP from a previous borrowing for the same purpose.

Let's assume that a young couple wants to buy their first home. They have their eye on a particular $200,000 resale condominium for which they will want at least a $10,000 down payment. They have only $4500 in savings, but they each have almost $8,000 in their individual RRSP's. Their incomes and minimal debt position easily qualify them for the necessary $190,000 mortgage.

Given this couple's minimal savings, they should not use any of that toward their down payment, to ensure they have enough cash on hand for the various *closing costs* associated with any home purchase. Instead, they can *each* consider borrowing $5,000 from their individual RRSP accounts to provide the full $10,000 down payment.

Great! They now have the necessary down payment. *But* they must keep in mind that, as with any debt, this must be repaid to their respective RRSP's, to a specific predetermined schedule.

Present legislation permits each first-time Buyer, as defined above, to borrow up to $20,000 from his RRSP, interest-free, to be used as a down payment on a home purchase. The total amount of this loan must be repaid over 15 years (at least 1/15 annually) beginning with the second year after the withdrawal is made. Any shortfall in the amount repaid in any year is taxed as normal income that year.

3. CLOSING COSTS

Cash-strapped first-time Buyers need to be particularly sensitive to the many *closing costs* associated with their home purchase. In those provinces that impose a **property transfer tax,** this can often be a Buyer's single largest closing cost.

Fortunately, the first-time Buyer *may* be eligible for a one-time *exemption.*

For example, in British Columbia, as of 2007, any first-time purchaser buying a home in Greater Vancouver, the Fraser Valley, or Victoria areas of the province may be exempt from this transfer tax, if the value of his purchase does not exceed $375,000. In all other areas of the province this exemption threshold is $265,000. (Note: British Columbia imposes other residency and mortgage amount qualifications before the Buyer is exempted from this tax.)

Wherever the Buyer resides in Canada, his alert Realtor should be up-to-date on the current rules and options that apply in his particular province.

....

Since our young couple is planning their condo purchase in Vancouver, and they qualify in all respects, they will be exempt from paying the normal $2,000 property transfer tax. However, all of the other traditional costs associated with closing a real estate transaction will still apply to them.

Fortunately, their $4,500 savings account will be more than adequate to cover these costs, and they can now look forward to moving into their first home.

Refer back to Chapter Eleven for details of closing costs.

A significant proportion of all home sales and purchases in Canada, particularly favoured by downsizing retirees, young professionals, and first-time Buyers, involves condominiums.

This section will provide an overview of this popular real estate product.

1. WHAT IS A CONDOMINIUM?

The word "condominium" does not describe a specific structural form. Rather it is the legal form or framework for a certain *category* of residential property.

Condominiums may be apartments, townhouses, duplexes and even detached houses, if they share a common access road ("Bare Land Strata"). Building lots, subdivisions and mobile home parks can also be classified as condominiums. The legal ownership form is referred to as **"strata ownership".**

Regardless of the type of unit, if it has been classified as a condominium, the project must be registered under the **Condominium Act** of the province in which it was constructed. Once registered, the project is brought into legal effect as a *Strata Corporation.*

The owner of a condominium will own the ***"unit"*** itself. This ownership interest will be legally registered in the owner's name, as is the case with any other owned property. Ownership interest, aside from the unit itself, will include a proportionate interest, in common with all other owners, of *all the common elements* of the complex. These common elements will generally include the actual land the units are built on, the private access roads, driveways, gardens, common rooms, recreation facilities, garages, and any other elements of the project which can be used and accessed by all owners. In some more elaborate projects this could even include for example, a golf course, a marina or a man-made lake. The proportionate interest of each owner is determined from the ratio of his unit's square footage to the total square footage of all units in the complex.

A **"Bare Land Strata"** project is similar to a normal building-lot subdivision. The residential units and the land on which each sits, is individually owned. The rest of the land belongs proportionately, as a common element, to all owners.

Each condominium project, once registered, must be governed by the owners in a manner that conforms to the **Condominium Act** of that particular province.

REMEMBER.....	**If you are an owner in a condominium complex, you *must* conform to, and abide by, all the by-laws, rules, and regulations which are approved by majority vote of the owners, within the framework established by the Condominium Act of the province.**

Each owner will be assessed an annual *"strata fee"*, usually payable monthly, which will represent his proportionate share of the common area **expense budget** approved for the current year. This can be fairly nominal in Bare Land Strata situations, but quite significant in other cases.

It would not be unusual for example, for the strata fee in an apartment condominium, in a city like Vancouver, to cost several hundred dollars monthly.

As with any property ownership, each owner is responsible for his own property taxes, reflecting the assessed value of both his unit and of his proportionate share of the common elements. As well, he must budget for his own household insurance and in most cases, his utilities. Insurance of the structures and lands is arranged by the strata corporation.

Some owners find this *collective management concept* rather restrictive and not to their taste. However, it does offer huge advantages for many owners. To list a few:

- Condominium projects usually make more efficient use of land than does the average single-family dwelling. Since land is a major component of the cost of any home, a home within a condominium project is usually less expensive to construct, and hence, more affordable.

- Many *first-time* Buyers can enter the home-ownership market through a reasonably priced condominium. They can build their equity in it until they can afford to sell it and purchase their first house.
- Condominium projects are particularly appealing to those who are downsizing and no longer wishing to look after their own property. The Strata Corporation will be responsible for all landscaping, and building and grounds maintenance issues for all owners.
- A home within a condominium project is typically more secure, and easier to leave for extended periods, with few worries for the individual owner.
- Many owners enjoy the enhanced social interaction which can be present within a typical condominium project.

Strata or condominium living suits many people very well, for one or more of these reasons. There are those however who do not adjust well to the collective rule-setting environment.

If contemplating strata ownership under a Condominium Act, the prudent Buyer will do his homework, *before* buying in.

It can be an extremely costly proposition to buy a condominium, only to realize shortly after moving in that this form of ownership is not for you. A resale soon after buying and moving into a condominium will almost certainly cost in the thousands of dollars!

Most homes, whether strata or not, are good *long-term investments*, but they rarely make money on a *quick* re-sale, especially given the significant selling costs associated with each transaction.

2. PURCHASING A CONDOMINIUM

The previously-listed advantages of purchasing a condominium are valid. However, the prospective Buyer of such a unit *must* take special care before entering into a firm Contract of Purchase and Sale. His due diligence will include:

a) **A careful review of the *minutes*** of at least the previous two years, of the Strata Corporation's Council Meetings, ensures that the potential Buyer is informed of all prospective or current problems which the owners have discussed at various meetings.

b) **A review of the current *financial statements*** of the Strata Corporation is equally imperative. A Buyer should know that the project has a healthy *reserve fund*, not only for planned, costly maintenance items such as pool renovations or exterior painting, but also for an unexpected major repair, such as a roof leak. In the absence of a sufficient reserve, all owners would have to pay in proportion to their ownership interest, a "special assessment" to fund the repair or replacement. This *could* amount to unplanned expenditures of thousands of dollars for each owner.

c) **A professional inspection** which is perhaps even more important than in the case of a single-family dwelling. It is preferable to retain an Inspector who specializes in condominium structures. A prospective Buyer should have not only the specific *unit* inspected, but also all of the *common area structures.* It is especially crucial to have the Inspector verify that there are no past or present moisture problems anywhere in the structure of the complex.

A lesson learned... Many condominium purchasers in the late 1980's and 1990's paid a heavy price for failing to do such structural inspections. During that period, special assessments of $25,000 to $100,000 ***per unit*** *became common-place for owners of condominiums, especially in the western coastal regions. Major, moisture-related remedial work on many complexes often ran into the millions of dollars.*

New building codes and construction techniques, along with government-mandated, new-home warranties provided by Builders, have greatly reduced this risk to Buyers of *new* condominiums.

The prudent Buyer however, will still want to be assured that no surprises lurk in the complex, of which he is about to become a part-owner.

3. CONDOMINIUM PURCHASING STRATEGIES

Virtually all of the strategies and approaches outlined in *Part III – THE BUYING PROCESS*, are also valid for the Buyer of a condominium.

The key exception is that **when making an offer on a condominium unit**, the Buyer should always add, in addition to his normal *financing and inspection* conditions, an extra condition along the following lines:

"Subject to the Buyer being satisfied with the results of his review of the minutes and financial statements of the Strata Corporation for the preceding twenty-four month period. This condition is for the sole benefit of the Buyer."

REMEMBER..... With careful due diligence, owning a strata unit within a well-run and properly-maintained condominium complex is a very practical form of home ownership for many.

An extra measure of investigation prior to making a firm commitment to purchase, will ensure that it becomes a happy, as well as profitable, experience.

4. CONDOMINIUM SELLING STRATEGIES

Many of the approaches outlined in *Part II – THE SELLING PROCESS*, are also valid for the sale of strata units within a condominium complex.

A few exceptions:

- The Seller should have readily available for his Realtor, *all* financial statements and minutes of meetings of the Strata Corporation, for at least the past two years.
- If a *Special Assessment* of the Strata Corporation is pending or has been assessed, the Seller should clearly indicate in the listing that *he* will pay his unit's portion of such assessment in full.
- A Seller must realize that the existence of a multitude of closely *comparable* units, and their listing and selling prices, makes it much easier for a Buyer and his Realtor to assess market value, than is the case for single-family dwellings, which tend to be very heterogeneous. *Realistic pricing is therefore extremely important.*
- In most communities, some Realtors tend to *specialize* in the sale of condominium properties. Because of the unique characteristics of these properties, a prudent Seller (or Buyer) should certainly include several such specialists in his list of potential Realtors, before making his selection of Realtor.

With over 200,000 new-home construction starts in Canada annually, a large component of all home sales involves the purchase of *newly-built* condominiums or single-family dwellings.

Both *Part III – THE BUYING PROCESS*, and *Part IV – BUYING OR SELLING A STRATA HOME*, laid out the basic logic and strategy leading a Buyer to a successful and hopefully, best-value purchase. Those foundations remain valid for a Buyer looking to purchase a newly-constructed home.

However, there are some unique issues to take into consideration when purchasing "*brand new*" is your objective:

- Any *new* home, be it single-family or condominium, purchased in Canada, is subject to GST being applied to the purchase price. As of July, 2007, GST stood at 6%.
- Many Buyers of such properties will qualify for a *partial* rebate of this tax, if the home they are purchasing does *not* exceed $450,000 in value. The rebate amount tops out at $7560, if the home price is under $350,000. For each $1000 of the purchase price above $350,000, the Buyer loses 1% of the $7560 maximum rebate, until it disappears altogether at a $450,000 purchase price.

  If our young couple were buying their $200,000 condominium apartment in a newly-built complex, they would have been eligible for the full $7560 rebate.

  The ***Canadian Home Builders' Association*** *and other groups regularly press the Federal Government to raise these rebate cut-off levels, to recognize the dramatic increases in home prices over the last decade. It would be wise for a new-home Buyer therefore, to tune himself in to the rules existing at the time of his contemplated purchase.*

Most Developers will allow a Buyer to assign *back* to the Developer, the amount of any rebate for which the Buyer qualifies. The Developer will then collect only the remaining difference owing on the GST, from the Buyer.

- Many Developers have their own *sales offices* to sell their project. Therefore, they often present their own *Contract of Purchase and Sale*, which they will ask a Buyer to sign if he wishes to purchase from them.

  BEWARE of what you sign! Many such contracts favour the Developer or Builder to an unreasonable degree. It is best in such situations for the Buyer to add a ***"subject to contract review by the Buyer's Lawyer"*** clause, when making an offer under such circumstances.

- Many Developers or Builders selling their own project will try to lead the Buyer to believe that the posted price is non-negotiable.

  Unless you are in the midst of a *hot* Seller's Market, don't believe it! **Negotiate!** Often the Seller will absorb the GST amount or even more.

REMEMBER..... Unless the Developer's project is substantially sold out, he will usually be very keen to make a deal with you.

- If however, you have selected a good Realtor to assist *you* in purchasing your newly-built home, he should be able to handle your negotiations for you and hopefully, add value on your behalf. Even if they are not listed with a Realtor, Builders realize that they must offer Realtors a commission in order to attract the Realtors' clients to the project. Many Developers choose to list their project with a Realtor in order to achieve MLS exposure.

- When purchasing a newly-built home, it is entirely reasonable for you to expect that there will be *no material deficiencies* in the home before you complete the transaction. Unlike a resale home, in which you have to expect a certain amount of normal wear and tear due to age, the Developer or Builder is selling you a *brand new home.*

A professional *inspection* is particularly crucial in helping you to identify *all* defects. List them for the Seller, and insist that they be remedied, prior to closing date, if at all possible.

- Developers and Builders are required by legislation in most provinces, to *provide third-party warranty insurance* to new-home Buyers. They are required to register and pay into a special insurance fund, for every project on which they receive a building permit. Check with your Realtor for details of this program in your province, and have your Lawyer carefully review the warranty undertakings, as part of his legal review of the contract.
- All provinces have a *Builders Lien Act* which obliges a Developer to hold back a portion of the contracted price of all improvements done by his contractor. This is meant to protect the owner of the property against any claims by subcontractors working on the project. In most provinces the specified holdback amount is 10% and the duration of holdback is 45 days after completion of the work. This is equal to the period during which any subcontractor may register a lien on the project for any moneys owed to him for labour or materials he supplied to the project.

  Although this is a statutory requirement that is imposed on each Developer or Builder, it is wise for the Buyer of a newly-constructed unit to *include a holdback* from his purchase price, for the dollar amount and period of time after completion date, as is specified in that province's Builders Lien Act. Your Realtor, Lawyer or Notary will be able to advise you on the specific legislation applicable in your province, as well as on the proper wording of such a clause.

  The purpose of this inclusion in your Contract of Purchase and Sale, is to ensure that *you* do not get caught with a lien on your newly-purchased home. This could, in some cases, be registered against the property even *after* your completion date has passed.

••••••••••••••••••••••••

As with purchasing a new car, buying a newly-built home can offer many rewards to its first owner, *as long* as he exercises extra care in the due diligence process, and includes all necessary conditions in his purchase offer.

REMEMBER.........If the Buyer's conditions are prudent and reasonable, and the Seller insists on seriously diluting them, the Buyer may be better off to walk away and keep looking!

Long term, your home is clearly an outstanding investment, and one of your very few avenues for increasing your net worth *tax-free*.

Generally we do not buy our home with *investment value* as our first concern. Our usual priority is to acquire our *own*, comfortable place in which to live. We want a home that suits our lifestyle in location, type, and character of dwelling.

Nevertheless, we should be mindful when purchasing a home, of the potential impact of certain decisions we may make, on the ***investment value*** of the home we select.

TYPICAL VALUE ENHANCERS

1. Location, Location, Location!

There is no question that location is a key driver of value. *Waterfront and view properties everywhere are the ultimate proof that the right location can pay huge dividends.*

Although a Buyer's family needs and financial circumstances place practical limits on choice of location, a few considerations should be kept in mind with respect to location:

- The least expensive home in an excellent neighbourhood has a greater *value growth* potential than others in the same area.
- Every community has known areas which are more desirable than others. Try to avoid the "problem" areas.
- Try for the best area that you can afford which still meets all of your *needs*.

2. Type of Home

Single-family dwellings tend to show far more financial appreciation over time, than do condominium properties. If financial circumstances require that you start out with a condominium property, use that investment as a springboard to a house as soon as you reasonably can.

I know a single mother of two in Victoria who started out with a $48,000, one-bedroom condo about 15 years ago. Two years later she upgraded to a $55,000 two-bedroom condo. Three years after that she bought a house for $208,000. Today that home is worth $550,000. Almost all of her equity growth came from the house.

3. Effective Use of Leverage

One of the very few "good" types of debt is the one incurred to *buy a home* of any type. As outlined in Chapter 10, it is much better to make monthly payments on a mortgage, than to pay roughly the same amount to a landlord.

A Buyer, able to borrow as much as 95% of the home's value, has the exciting prospect of growing his *net worth* dramatically through:

- Paying off every month, an increasing portion of the principal owing;
- Participation in the long-term appreciation of his own real estate investment.

Very few investments can beat the kind of returns Canadians have seen in real estate over the past 50 years. And remember, in Canada ***all capital appreciation on your primary residence is tax-exempt.***

Add to this the potential to make your mortgage interest payments tax-deductible in certain circumstances, as outlined by Fraser Smith in his book, "Is Your Mortgage Tax Deductible?" The result may be an investment vehicle that is truly exceptional.

4. Asset Improvement

Most of us know of someone who has made a lot of money by buying a "tired" house in a good location, and strategically upgrading it to enhance its appeal and value. You can do the same, with creativity, a lot of elbow-grease, and some investment.

5. Time

Probably the single-largest value enhancer for your home is ***time.*** In 1960 you could buy a very nice house in Canada for $15,000. By 1980, an average home cost about $80,000. By 2007, the average was close to $300,000.

Many Canadians who several decades ago, bought modest homes on modest incomes, have become financially very well-off in later years, largely as a result of this early, and subsequent, investments in their various homes.

REMEMBER..... Your home is not only your "castle", but also your major net worth builder. It is one of the finest *long-term personal investments* you are likely to make.

POSTSCRIPT

Throughout this guide to enhancing both your home-buying and home-selling experience, I have made every effort to ensure that the suggested approaches remain relevant for many years to come.

Nevertheless, occasional facts and statistics are derived from provincial or federal statutes which existed at the date of publication. You, the reader, must ensure that you update yourself on any relevant changes which subsequently may have been enacted. Any Realtor should be current on the legislation applicable in your province.

....

I welcome your input. Your comments regarding this guide's relevance and value to you, as an aspiring or existing homeowner, will be most appreciated, and will prove helpful in subsequent reprints of this book.

Please direct your comments via e-mail to:
peterdolezal@thenakedhomeowner.com

APPENDICES

- **REALTOR RATING WORKSHEET**
- **COMMISSION SIDE LETTER**
- **CALCULATION OF NET PROCEEDS OF SALE**
- **GROSS DEBT SERVICE CALCULATION**
- **TOTAL DEBT SERVICE CALCULATION**

APPENDIX 1

REALTOR RATING WORKSHEET

	Suggested Scale	*Your* Adjusted Scale	REALTOR **A**	REALTOR **B**	REALTOR **C**
LISTING PRESENTATION:					
PRICING LOGIC	0 - 20				
ADVERTISING PLAN	0 - 20				
WEBSITE PLAN	0 - 20				
OPEN HOUSE FREQUENCY	0 - 20				
PHOTOGRAPH PLAN	0 - 10				
PROFESSIONAL FLOOR PLANS	0 - 10				
OPEN HOUSE ADVERTISING	0 - 10				
COMMISSION STRUCTURE	0 - 10				
COMMISSION SIDE LETTER	0 - 10				
OTHER FACTORS:					
ENTHUSIASM	0 - 20				
GOOD LISTENER	0 - 20				
AREA FAMILIARITY	0 - 10				
AREA SUCCESS	0 - 10				
STAGING ADVICE	0 - 10				
FEEDBACK PLAN	0 - 10				
REFERENCES	0 - 10				
GOOD COMMUNICATOR	0 - 10				
PROFESSIONAL APPEARANCE	0 - 10				
YOUR COMFORT LEVEL	0 - 10				
TOTAL SCORE	MAX. 250				

1. Adjust the Rating Scale to reflect *your priorities*.
2. Score each item from 0 to 10 or 20, where 0 is the worst score.
3. The relative total scores will rank the candidate Realtors.
4. Select the Realtor who is clearly superior. If several are close in total scores, choose the Realtor with whom you are most comfortable.

IF YOUR HIGHEST-SCORING REALTOR SCORES BELOW 200, CONSIDER INTERVIEWING ADDITIONAL REALTORS!

APPENDIX 2

COMMISSION SIDE LETTER

June 1, 2007

Dear *(Homeowner's Name)*:

This letter will confirm our agreement that, notwithstanding the commission structure set out in the Listing Agreement dated May 31, 2007, we have agreed that the commission will be reduced in the following circumstances, by the amounts specified:

1. If your sale completes without the involvement of any Realtor aside from myself, the total commission payable will be reduced by $2,000.

2. Should you enter, with my assistance, into a firm commitment to purchase a replacement home, and do so prior to the date of completion of the sale of your home, your commission payable will be reduced by $1,000.

3. Should both events occur, as set out in #1 and #2 above, your commission will be reduced by both amounts, for a total reduction of $3,000.

Yours sincerely,

(*John Smith*)
(*ABC REALTY*)

***(NOTE**: For a particularly high value listing which approaches or exceeds $1 million, the $2,000 reduction in #1 might quite reasonably be increased to $3,000.)*

APPENDIX 3

CALCULATION OF NET PROCEEDS OF SALE

SELLING PRICE $________

COST OF SELLING

Commission Payable	$________	
GST on Commission	$________	
Home Preparation	$________	
Staging	$________	
Legal	$________	
Property Tax/Utilities Adjustment	$________	
Moving	$________	
TOTAL SELLING COSTS	$________	$________

NET PROCEEDS AVAILABLE FOR NEXT HOUSE $________

APPENDIX 4

GROSS DEBT SERVICE (GDS) CALCULATION

GROSS Monthly Household Income: $__________

~ Multiply by 32% Allowable for Housing $__________

DEDUCT:

Estimated Monthly Property Taxes $_______________
Estimated Monthly Utilities $_______________
1/2 Monthly Strata Fee - *if Condo* $_______________

TOTAL DEDUCTIONS: $__________

TOTAL AVAILABLE MONTHLY FOR MORTGAGE PAYMENTS: $

NOTE: If a Buyer is otherwise debt-free, front-line Lenders, such as Banks, Credit Unions, or Trust Companies, will:

1) In the case of a conventional mortgage, where the Buyer's down payment is at least 20% of the appraised value of the property being purchased, consider the 32% allowable for housing to be merely a guideline which can, in some circumstances, be exceeded.

2) In the case of a high-ratio mortgage, the 32% ceiling is rigidly applied, without exception.

APPENDIX 5

TOTAL DEBT SERVICE (TDS) CALCULATION

GROSS Monthly Household Income: $_______________

Multiply by 40% Allowable for Housing & All Other Debts $_______________

DEDUCT Monthly Household Debt Payments:

Automobile	$_______________
Credit Cards	$_______________
Line of Credit	$_______________
Student Loans	$_______________
Other Loans	$_______________

TOTAL MONTHLY DEBT PAYMENTS (Subtract) $_______________

GROSS MONTHLY $$ AVAILABLE FOR HOUSING $_______________

DEDUCT MONTHLY HOUSING COSTS:

Estimated Property Tax	$_______________
Estimated Monthly Utilities	$_______________
1/2 Estimated Monthly Strata Fee, *if Condo*	$_______________

$_______________

NET MONTHLY INCOME AVAILABLE FOR MORTGAGE PAYMENTS $_______________

NOTE: If a Buyer is otherwise debt-free, front-line Lenders, such as Banks, Credit Unions or Trust Companies, will:

1) In the case of a conventional mortgage, where the Buyer's down payment is at least 20% of the appraised value of the property being purchased, consider the 40% allowable for housing and all other debts, to be merely a guideline which can, in some circumstances, be exceeded.

2) In the case of a high-ratio mortgage, the 40% ceiling is rigidly applied, without exception.

ISBN 142512521-2

9 781425 125219